THE HEART
OF RELATIONSHIPS

105 TRUTHS ON THE PATH
TO INTIMACY

JOHN THOMAS WOOD

Booktrope Editions
Seattle, WA 2014

Cover Design by Ewelina Nowakowska

Edited by Magdalen Powers

PRINT ISBN 978-1-62015-357-4

EPUB ISBN 978-1-62015-382-6

Library of Congress Control Number: 2014905641

TABLE OF CONTENTS

INTRODUCTION

MOST DAYS, I BELIEVE LEARNING ABOUT LOVE is all that we are here for. If this is true, it explains why we have such a tough time getting our arms around love, marriage, and intimate relationships. Love is mysterious, pervasive, changing, and elusive. We worship for love, we die for it, we travel on a long journey to arrive at love, and often we rail against it, cursing, asking questions and retreating from that which we seek.

Learning to love may seem easy at first, when we fall in love, and later it may seem the hardest thing we have ever done. Our desire for love demands from us our most patient, most creative abilities, and our pursuit of love seems just as likely to draw us into the shadows and mug us as it is to lead us to the light.

Love is a paradox. The rules seem to say that we have to be in full possession of our unique, individual selves and, at the same time, let go and surrender, giving and holding nothing back. How is that possible? How can we walk such a tightrope and pay attention to anything else? It is one of the glorious miracles of our lives that love happens at all, that despite our greed, fear, pain, and alienation, we still give ourselves to love, sometimes once, sometimes over and over again.

We seem to seek something we cannot possibly have, and, one day without warning, we wake up and find that it has come to our bedside. Love has arrived. We are indeed blessed. Then, as if waking from a dream, we discover that love is gone. Was it an illusion? Did we really have anything? Or were we allowed to visit for a while, to merely ride along on the river of love for part of our journey?

Love happens, is born within us and dies, changes, deepens—if we're fortunate—and maybe even takes over our lives. And while much of this process is a mystery, there is one thing we know about love: it happens in relationship. It has a subject and an object. Love always has a lover and a beloved.

The convenient thing is, we are always in some kind of relationship, so there is always the opportunity to learn about our loving. Knowing as much as we can about these relationships and learning from them seems to be more of a challenge than ever. Relationships today have assumed an importance and an emphasis that our parents and certainly our grandparents would not have dreamed of. For many of us, relationships are the spiritual path we will walk. It is in our love relationships that we will work hard on our personal growth, discover our own depths, and move closer to the spirit world. Relationships challenge us to free ourselves from old ways of thinking that no longer serve us, to be aware of our blind spots, and to develop our unique personal power. It is in our intimate relationships that we wake up and discover who we are.

That's why I've written *The Heart of Relationships*. Maybe enough has been written about love. Maybe. But I cannot help but hope that I have something new to offer the person who is about to be married, about to be unmarried, or who is dancing the dance of intimacy, whether it's for the first time or the tenth. I set out to capture something about the way people relate to one another in intimate relationships and get as close as I could to *The Heart of Relationships*.

This book looks at the *how* of intimacy, a kind of "The Way Things Work" about close relationships, a book about thoughts, feelings, desires, and the consequences of our behaviors, a book about the "interpersonal physics" of relationships.

The Heart of Relationships marks the path to intimacy with 105 aphorisms. You might think of them as signposts along the way. I think this is a format that will increase learning and staying power. It's my hope that readers will remember the short, pithy headlines, once they've read the explanation, and will be able to apply many of the aphorisms to their intimate relationships. So when I say, for instance, "The lack of reciprocity is an early warning sign in all relationships," I give you an explanation of what reciprocity is, how it works, and why it's so important. Then you'll know for yourself how it applies to you and your partner.

Warning: this book may seem unromantic to you. It is, by design. I've tried to separate romance from love, from marriage, and from intimacy. They are all separate subjects to me. Allow me to tell you some things about the ways we relate and grow to love each other, and you supply the romance you want to your own encounters.

This book is not foolproof and is certainly not complete. I invite you to use it as a workbook, adapting the lessons for your own use, changing it and adding your own aphorisms along the way. Make it yours. And share it.

I invite your feedback.

JOHN THOMAS WOOD

1. THE MOST IMPORTANT RELATIONSHIP YOU HAVE IS THE RELATIONSHIP YOU HAVE WITH YOURSELF.

IF YOU HAVE TO SAY THIS CLICHÉ to yourself 10,000 times in order to make it real, do so. It's that important.

The story of your life will be a travelogue about your journey to yourself. The most important "jobs" you have on this planet will be this exploration of yourself and the formation of relationships with others.

You've heard this over and over in a different way: love yourself first, then love another. Is loving yourself narcissistic? Self-absorbed? We get a little confused when we talk about loving ourselves. That's one reason I say it differently: have yourself, know who you are and what you want, and treat yourself with respect. Then you will be able to fully give yourself to a relationship with another human being. To the extent you do not have yourself, you will look for the missing pieces in the other. This will a.) keep you out of a healthy relationship or b.) gradually erode the relationship you have.

Men and women who have unhealthy relationships with themselves have unhealthy relationships with others. When you surrender completely to another person or to a relationship, you abandon the essential core, the individual voice that is the basis of all authentic existence.

Only knowledge of self and acceptance of self will allow you to be free. This, in turn, allows you to be fully committed in a healthy relationship. Paradox? Believe it.

2. EVENTUALLY YOUR PARTNER COMES TO REGARD YOU AS YOU REGARD YOURSELF.

I'M GOING TO FIND IT HARD TO LOVE YOU if you hate yourself. This aphorism is a close relative of rule #1. It is difficult to love someone who believes they are unlovable. Such a woman or man will continually leave land mines in the road to intimacy, just in order to prove their point: "See, I knew you wouldn't love me; I was right all along."

What you believe to be true about yourself leads to what you value, or don't value, about yourself. This in turn leads to how you feel about yourself. These things are pervasive; they ooze out of your pores and surround you. They can be without words. They are powerful signals, powerful enough to convince anyone around you of your own picture of yourself. Therefore, when you believe that you are unlovable, unworthy, weak, or needy and don't deserve a lasting relationship, others will eventually adopt that belief about you, too.

You can—through your behavior and your messages to your partner—eventually convince this person across from you in the relationship that you aren't worth a damn. Self-defeating? You bet. It's as if some low, ugly part of you that hides in your personal swamp wants to be proven right; then it can be left alone.

Hiding behind that, and often very difficult to see, is the self that wants badly to be loved.

3. WHEN YOU LOSE TOUCH WITH THE CORE VOICE WITHIN YOU, YOUR RELATIONSHIPS WILL FLOUNDER.

THIS IS THE ESSENTIAL AND NECESSARY FIRST RULE for being powerful, for yourself, and for your loving relationships: listen to your own voice. Learn to listen to and respect your intuition, your logic, your feelings, your opinions, the voice of your spirit, and the voice inside that has always wanted to say, "_____."

Finding your voice, if it has been lost, respecting it, and speaking it is a very big deal. Start with the basic assumption, even if you have learned differently, that what you see, think, feel, and want is just as important as what anyone else does. Many of us have grown up with the idea that our job in life is to make other people happy.

There is joy in serving others, but that joy does not come until you "have" yourself to give. You cannot give, cannot truly serve if you are empty, depleted, without resources, and not getting your own needs met. Losing touch with your own inner voice means you are not being, or becoming, who you were meant to be. Eventually, this will distort any relationship of which you are a part.

The aim and purpose of your life is to unfold and become as loving and powerful as you can be, according to your own nature. Betray your own voice, and you betray your relationships.

4. EVERYTHING ABOUT YOU REFLECTS THE LEVEL OF LOVE YOU HAVE FOR YOURSELF.

YOU ARE A WALKING, TALKING, BREATHING EXHIBIT of the amount of love you have for yourself and, by extension, for others.

How you treat your body, how you dress, how your groom yourself, how you move, your facial expressions, the condition of your personal environment, how you speak—everything about you reflects the quality of the relationship you have with yourself. What you give and provide yourself—rest, good food, meaningful work, creativity, play, involvement with others, health care, time for yourself—all speak to the level of love that you provide for yourself. This is what you bring to someone else: your consciousness about who you are and the respect you have for yourself.

If you abuse yourself, you are likely to abuse others. If you neglect yourself, you will have a level of neglect for others. If you regard your body as a temple and your spirit as open and loving, you will look at others in the same way.

Take some time to assess what kind of statement you make, not just with your appearance but with your whole countenance and demeanor. What would you like to change that would reflect more self-love and love for others?

5. THE FIRST STEP IN IDENTIFYING AND MEETING THE NEEDS OF ANY GIVEN RELATIONSHIP IS TO ADDRESS YOUR OWN NEEDS.

"HOW CAN I BE YOURS? I am not even mine!" Voltaire has a character say. He is writing about meeting your own needs and 'having yourself' before you try to meet the needs of someone else.

How can you be in a healthy, happy relationship if half of the relationship is not getting its needs met? Your half. Who is going to best take care of you? You are. Who is going to know what you need if you don't? No one.

Many people will not live by this rule because if they do, they think of themselves as selfish. "Selfish" is a big horrible word for a lot of people. Most of us have grown up with strong admonishments from parents about being selfish.

Too many of us throw the baby out with the bathwater and overcorrect on the issue of being selfish. Being selfish is thinking and acting *only* on your own needs. The healthy person looks after her own needs first and then is an infinitely better position to respond to the wants and needs of those close to her. Know what you want. Know what you need. Act on it. Any meaningful relationship grows when both people are acting responsibly to meet their own needs and paying attention to the other as well.

If you neglect your own needs, who will meet them? If your own needs are not met, what will happen to you? Disappointment will surely follow if you expect others to discover and meet your needs when you have not.

6. WHEN I FEEL SECURE IN MYSELF, I AM FREE TO EXPERIENCE YOU AS YOU REALLY ARE.

YOU WILL SEE IN ANOTHER PART OF THIS BOOK that having a strong, individual sense of self is one of four key factors in maintaining a satisfying relationship. When I do have that sense of myself, I can fully see you for who you are. Feeling secure in myself, I can look out at you and see you without the filters of fear, manipulation, desire, or dependency.

Otherwise, I am, at some point, going to resort to a defensive posture, defending some part of me that is threatened by you. Not having a secure sense of who I am, I will fear your changes, your learning, and the other interests you have. I may subtly try to control you with threats or anger. I may withdraw, physically or emotionally.

When I fully see myself, when I fully have myself, I can put my self-interests aside and give my full attention to you.

7. No one can read your mind.

IF THIS IS SO GLARINGLY OBVIOUS, why does it still happen—every day—that one partner expects the other to know what they think, feel, or want? People will say to each other: "You knew what I wanted!" or "We never do it this way, you know that!" or "Doesn't it ever occur to you that I might want to _____?"

Can you hear the anger in those remarks? Somehow, we are disappointed, maybe hurt, that our partner is unable to understand our thoughts and feelings without our having given them a clear, specific voice. Why do we have to say everything? Because we cannot read minds or hearts, and because we change.

My own opinion about those folks who expect you to read their minds is that they're reluctant to say what they want. It's a risk to come right out and say specifically what you want. You may think it's selfish. You may not want to hear "no." In addition, many people think that asking their partner for what they want changes the nature of the transaction; it makes it less romantic. If I have to ask you to bring me flowers, it's not nearly as sweet as if you had surprised me. But if you're going to wait to be surprised, you're going to take the risk of being surprised in a way you don't appreciate.

There is the distinct possibility that saying how you feel and asking for what you want in a direct, specific way will be more romantic than you've ever imagined.

8. FREEDOM IN A RELATIONSHIP IS DIRECTLY RELATED TO TOLERANCE FOR CONFLICT.

I BET YOU'VE NEVER THOUGHT OF FREEDOM and conflict together. To the extent that a couple can bring conflict into the open and resolve issues on an ongoing basis, partners will increase their freedom. To the extent that conflict is avoided or unresolved, they will find themselves restricted.

When two people meet and form a relationship, their individual differences gradually emerge. Conflict springs from bringing these differences together. There are several ways people deal with conflict, many of them nonproductive: we deny conflict exists, avoid it, withdraw from dialogue, placate others involved, compromise, attack, and sometimes even attempt to creatively resolve it.

Some see a picture of conflict as always accompanied by stress, argument, and increased responsibility; they believe the absence of conflict is an indication of harmony. They trade conflict for what they believe is tranquility. A greater, deeper harmony—with freedom—exists if couples address conflict openly and creatively.

When we are able to bring our differences clearly and cleanly into the open and learn about each other, we have the real possibility of increasing our understanding, acceptance, and intimacy. We also increase the range of behavior that we allow for our partner and ourselves because we see that our partner's actions are separate and emerge from his or her individual identity.

If, however, differences (conflicts) are a threat and consistently raise fear in the relationship, both individuals will separately and as a unit try to subdue conflict. Conflict, and the ensuing dialogue which would bring more understanding, is controlled, and the thinking and behavior of each partner is brought under pressure to conform. Thus, individual freedom, which is the basis for the life of the relationship, is eroded.

This is a very common recipe for stagnant relationships.

9. THE UNKNOWN IN OURSELVES IS BOUND UP IN RELATIONSHIP TO OTHERS.

ONE OF THE REASONS YOU REMAIN FRAGMENTED, fail to speak from your core values, and do not achieve wholeness as a person is that you don't fully know yourself. One of the reasons you don't know yourself is that you have not spent any amount of quality time alone.

Solitude gives us the opportunity to find out deeply who we are, without the constant reference to another. We discover something about ourselves without the desires, needs, and feedback of our partner altering our perception.

As a therapist, I saw single or "unattached" clients regularly come in to do some meaningful work on themselves, only to stop that work when they got in relationship. The new love takes the interest, the attention, and, from their point of view, the need to go any deeper into their individual patterns and nonproductive behavior. It's nearly an admission that their interest in personal growth is only in order to form a relationship, and then all their problems will be solved.

There is no doubt that you do discover something about yourself in a significant relationship. But the deeper, less accessible parts of yourself go undiscovered when you are devoting all of your attention to a relationship, especially when that relationship is more superficial, more conflicted, and less satisfying than you are capable of.

Many couples seek comfort with each other and, in that comfort, give up the journey to learn more about themselves.

10. ONE OF THE MOST PROFOUND EXPERIENCES WE HAVE IS TO IDENTIFY IN ANOTHER THE ORIGIN OF OUR OWN JOY.

IN THE BEGINNING—that is, when we first start to breathe air—we fall in love. We see in our mother's eyes, face, and very presence that we make someone else happy and that we are made happy by them. This is bliss. We are peaceful and content; we are nurtured by another and we see that, outside of ourselves, someone is "causing" this. We see that another human being can, and is, giving us something profound and pervasive. We are loved and we love back.

This tête-à-tête with mom does not last forever and, depending on our circumstances, may be yanked away from us much too soon for our liking. Nevertheless, we remember it, at some level. Some thinkers say that we spend the rest of our lives hunting for this feeling in another person. The important thing seems to be that we feel, or have, enough of this love so we can stand on our own, giving and receiving joy in a more or less mutual exchange and not looking for the person who will simply give us this feeling as Mom did.

Yet, this is a large part of falling in love: to gaze into someone else's eyes and see the reflection of your own love gazing back at you. It can make a lot of things right.

11. COMPASSION ARRIVES WHEN YOU HAVE ACCEPTED YOUR OWN "UNDESIRABLE" QUALITIES.

WHEN YOU HAVE LOOKED INTO YOUR OWN NATURE long enough and hard enough to see your own imperfect humanness and to accept it, you have the beginning of a genuine sense of compassion. After you have done battle with your own demons and learned to accept qualities that you previously found ugly, negative, or shameful, you can give that gift to another.

On the other hand, if you have remained blind to your own anger, fear, or shame, you may not recognize or accept those qualities in your partner (or friends). Learning to "feel fully with yourself," to know and accept your own qualities, precedes a full compassion for others.

True understanding and acceptance of someone else starts with giving that kind of love to yourself. To love someone else, you must love yourself first. To understand someone else deeply, you must first understand yourself. How is it that you could escape being a part of the human race?

Some people are stymied here because they think of loving themselves or being compassionate to themselves as selfish. Selfishness is a trap, to be sure, but the fear of being selfish may keep more of us from genuine self-love than need be.

It is one of life's more important balancing acts to find the right recipe for mixing compassion and understanding of yourself with that of another.

12. WE ALL MAKE A JOURNEY TO THE OTHER SIDE; THE BOAT IS NOT THE JOURNEY.

ALL OF US MAKE A JOURNEY across a sea, our life journey, which we will make regardless of the partner we have chosen. That journey is our own. When we choose a relationship, we are choosing a boat in which to make the journey. That relationship may be with a person, your god, or your calling in life.

It's important to know the difference between the journey and the boat. Knowing the difference leads to self-responsibility, perspective, and putting your priorities in order. The boat (your partner) bears no responsibility for your journey; it does not determine your direction, your speed, your port of arrival, or the quality of the voyage. It certainly may influence those things, but it is not in charge of your journey. You are responsible for your own journey. And, remember, you chose the boat.

Row, row, row your boat, gently down the stream. Merrily, merrily, merrily, merrily, life is but a dream.

13. THE DESIRE FOR RELATIONSHIP IS INNATE; THE ABILITY TO MAINTAIN ONE IS LEARNED.

ALL OF US ARE BORN WITH THE URGE to merge with another human being. The species would not last long if we did not have a strong hankering to find a mate and reproduce. Relationships satisfy another need, too: we are a gregarious species, and we all need to affiliate, to form friendships and join groups. The ways and means of forming a relationship and keeping it going are altogether different matters, however. We learn "relationship competency" and we learn it in an informal and largely unconscious way...many times after the failure of one or more important relationships.

It's curious, when you think about it. We've accepted the fact that nearly everyone needs to take trigonometry in school, despite the fact that a small percentage of us use it, but we do not spend much of our time and resources on teaching children about relationships, including marriage. We keep looking at the incredibly high rate of divorces, shaking our heads, and doing nothing about it—nothing as far as public education goes, that is.

Okay, off the soapbox. I want to emphasize the fact that we all go through a learning process about keeping a relationship healthy and that the learning is not nearly as deliberate and conscious as it could be. All of us could profit if we devoted more of our young years to learning how to love someone else, efficiently, thoroughly, perpetually, and with gusto.

Where do we learn the way we love? In the family. In that first delicate decade of life, we learn the basics of relating to another person with love and affection. We spend the rest of our life refining those lessons.

RELATIONSHIP
ISSUES

THE HEART OF RELATIONSHIPS   23

14. WE INVENT OUR PARTNERS.

WHAT KIND OF COCKAMAMIE IDEA is this? Don't our partners have a past and a future—a life—all their own? How can we "invent" the person we love? Read on.

In our adolescence and into our twenties, we are busy with the future. It is a time ripe with anticipation, expectation, and idealization. We see that the future lies ahead of us like a long, four-lane freeway, and we can do with it what we want. In no area of our lives is this truer than in our intimate relationships. We have specific desires, we expect certain things of our mate, and we have a dream of what our relationship—and, often, our family—will look like. This picture we have of the way things will be (or "should" be) is very strong and, for the most part, not in our conscious awareness. This is our invented partner.

Into this paint-by-the-numbers dream walks another person, unsuspecting, with a picture of her own. Often we don't see this person because our projected picture of our ideal mate is so pervasive. In addition, if we were to see the real person behind our projection, we might have to deal with the loss of our ideal mate. But things do change.

Living together day in and day out gradually wears out the projection, and our image of our partner changes as the real and, perhaps, ordinary person emerges. This is when we wake up and say: "Who the hell did I marry?" This "collision" of the ideal partner and the real partner is often a crisis in a relationship, especially if our projection was strong and far removed from reality. The loss of our ideal mate is a great loss...often too great for the relationship to stand.

There is an important lesson in all this, a coming to consciousness out of pain. We can see that our desire was a dream, that our expectations kept us from seeing someone as they really are, and that idealization is not reality.

There is a fine line between trying to change a person into who you badly want them to be and creating the kind of relationship you want with a real person. That person has their own ideas of who they are and what they want.

15. PEOPLE FORM RELATIONSHIPS "IN ORDER TO..."

WE DON'T THINK MUCH ABOUT IT, or we simply say, "We're in love." But we form relationships for a reason. We get together with others in order to get something done, to accomplish a life dream or resolve an issue involving our personal growth. For most of us, this goal is below our level of consciousness, and we think of our relationship as an arrival point. More often than not, our relationships are a means to something else.

It's useful to ask questions such as: "What do I hope to accomplish with this relationship?" "How will we do that?" "What do I really want from my partner?" "What do the two of us want together?" "What happens when we finish our individual and mutual goals?" "What would it be like to just *be* with this person, without a career, a family, or a home?"

Finding a good father for your children, ending loneliness, building a business, beginning a family, building a home, having a steady source of affection or sex, helping someone else, escaping some other situation...all are goals that relationships might have. Often we are in a relationship in order to complete, or work through, one of our own life issues. We may need to learn one of our life lessons in a relationship: realizing that we rescue others, working out of a victim mentality, knowing ourselves more deeply, developing interpersonal skills, or stepping into our own power.

Clarify, as best you can, what you really want and the reasons for your relationship continuing. Perhaps the "purest" of relationships are those where we want or need nothing from the other but simply like to be together.

16. RELATIONSHIPS ARE FORMED FOR DIFFERENT REASONS THAN A GENERATION AGO.

OUR GRANDPARENTS FORMED INTIMATE RELATIONSHIPS and got married (or probably vice versa) in order to build a family and a home together, to stay together for life, in an institution called marriage. Marriage is no longer just an institution that "houses" reproduction, shelter, family alliances, and the future work force. Past generations formed relationships without the same kinds of demands and expectations that we have for close relationships today. If, a hundred years ago, people wanted to explore the deeper meaning of life or engage in an ongoing process of personal discovery, they probably entered the monastery, devoted themselves to a spiritual life, or entered long-term psychotherapy. We make a mistake when we believe we can—or should—have the same kind of relationship as our grandparents or our parents did.

Today, many people have a very high expectation of an intimate relationship—that the relationship becomes the crucible for awakening our deepest nature, that, as Marianne Williamson puts it, "relationships exist to hasten our walk to God." Many of us get into a relationship with the explicit agenda of having it foster our personal growth and that of our partner—quite different than our grandparents would have dreamed of.

This can put unreasonable pressure on a relationship, if somehow I expect my relationship to "pay off" for me individually, to be the place where I get my personal growth needs met. While it may be true that in many relationships our partner helps us grow and change, it is not our partner's responsibility to make that happen. Blaming the relationship itself for our own failure to move ahead in life and make the changes we want is only a denial of our own responsibility and power.

On the other hand, a mutual devotion to a close relationship and a shared consciousness of what intimacy can bring in spiritual terms can fulfill an exciting promise. Willingness to learn and enough personal skill can bring significant individual growth and a spiritual awakening.

Today it is truer than ever that we are inventing and reinventing social institutions to be a part of, certainly including marriage. That is both challenging and exciting.

17. SHE IS NOT WHAT SHE IS TO YOU; SHE IS WHAT SHE IS.

ONE DAY WHILE STANDING IN LINE at the post office, I realized that my partner's purpose in life had little to do with being my partner. It was one of those moments, born out of naiveté, when a simple truth becomes profound. I saw that who she was had much less to do with our relationship than I previously believed. She had a life before me and would have a life after me; she had her own full identity that had nothing to do with me, and her life would follow its own course.

Before you start trashing me for not realizing this before I was 12 years old (when I thought my parents' sole purpose was to be my parents), think about it. When we are in a long-term relationship with another, we began to think that the other's identity is wrapped up with ours. She is "my wife" or he's "my husband." Of course, we do this all the time with "our children."

Most of the time, we determine what the other person is as they relate to us and as we want them to relate to us. We hold them up to this mirror, and the mirror says at the top: "What I want you to be." Or even "What you said you would be." You get the picture. We forget that our partner—no matter how intimate we are or how long we've been together or how well we think we know them—is a separate human being. We forget that, or we ignore it because it serves us.

Our urges to have things work the way we want, to fill in the spaces in our carefully laid-out dreams, are so strong that we fail to acknowledge the separate and distinctly different identity of our partner. Remember, even though you are in this wonder-filled relationship together, you are separate human beings and have different reactions, ideas, feelings, values, and beliefs about life. Try to step back and look at your partner as someone who doesn't know you. Who are they then?

18. A HEALTHY RELATIONSHIP IS NOT TWO HALVES COMING TOGETHER TO MAKE A WHOLE.

THE SENTIMENT THAT THE TWO OF US together make a whole is reflected in many popular songs as well as in many more love letters. This feeling also influences our divorce statistics. It is not the stuff of healthy relationships.

Some psychotherapists call this idea "the fusion model," in that you and your partner basically believe that you are incomplete by yourselves and that by fusing with another person who is also incomplete, you make a pretty darn good whole person. One half and one half makes one. Or 60 percent and 40 percent make a 100-percent guarantee of a loving relationship. But relationships built on that belief—conscious or not—usually cannot stand the weight of two people depending too much on each other.

This kind of relationship eventually begins to buckle because two people are extracting too much of their well-being from the fact that the bonding has to be there and has to be good. The feeling is that things can't go wrong. The relationship is especially susceptible to conflict avoidance, to threat from outside friendships, and to ongoing illness or "ill being" in one of the partners.

A whole person meeting a whole person makes for a strong relationship. If our expectation is that we are going to become whole once we are joined with another, we are going to be disappointed.

19. LISTENING IS THE FUEL OF ANY GOOD RELATIONSHIP.

LISTENING IS CRITICAL—maybe half of what you need to know. Listening deeply conveys a sense of respect, builds empathy and compassion, and leads to intimacy. Any relationship based on listening—business, friendship, or love—will be a great relationship. Ignore this at your peril.

There is a lot to learn about listening, an underappreciated art. I'll leave you with just a few things.

Decide to listen. Make it an intention when your partner speaks, and if you can't listen right then, say so. Listening takes energy.

Listen not just to words. Listen to voice—tone, rhythm, pace, volume, emphasis, strength, and weakness. Listen to silences and what is not said. Report what you hear and what you don't hear.

Listen, watch, sense...nonverbal expression. We also speak with our eyes, face, body, hands, hips, walk, eyebrows...you get the idea. Sometimes I think our whole person speaks, not just our mouths. Pay attention; this is often a more powerful message than the words. And sometimes it doesn't match the words at all.

Listen with empathy and compassion. Put yourself behind the other's words and expressions to see what it is like to be them for a moment or two. This will help you, and them, in leaps and bounds. It is marvelous to have someone truly understand and empathize with you. This is good soul food.

Let your partner know that you listening. Acknowledge them and confirm what they are saying.

Learn how your partner wants to be listened to and what they want from you when you are listening. We are different. Some want silence; others want some verbal expression to know that you're following them.

Finally, put yourself aside when you listen. Tuck away your opinions, feelings, laughter, sarcasm, wants, needs, and judgments when you really want to listen to another.

You don't have to sacrifice yourself to be a good listener, just suspend your self-interest while you hear someone else, and find out what his or her life is like in this moment. Whenever you find yourself in trouble with each other, make a resolution to deeply listen to the other.

Good listening is nearly a miracle.

20. THE DEEPEST WOUND WE INFLICT ON OUR LOVE MAY NOT BE NEGLECT BUT INTENSE SCRUTINY.

SOMETIMES THE PRESSURE TO BE all you can be, resolve every issue, stay very close, and reach the full potential of the relationship can be too much. Sometimes the scrutiny, the pressure, and the unyielding attention turn out to be a vise instead of a salve.

There are individuals who, in an intimate relationship, insist that every issue get resolved, every conflict be dealt with, and every slip of tongue or behavior be thoroughly interpreted. And there are couples that are continually involved in examining the process of their relationship, what it means, and how it could be improved. Too much attention can be unhealthy absorption.

I can't overestimate the value and the power that comes with awareness, insight, and clear communications skills, but too much attention, intensity, and self-examination may spring from fear and, at least, can get awfully tiresome. There is a good chance that this kind of pressure could destroy the very love it is aimed at preserving.

Sometimes I think of relationship issues like I think about the common cold: With lots of medication, you get over a cold in seven days. If you take nothing, you get over it in a week.

Talking and endless processing of issues can be a drain without some kind of resolution or action. Let some things be. Save your resources for the issues that count, and deal with them in the best time and place you can.

21. THE LACK OF RECIPROCITY IN A RELATIONSHIP IS AN EARLY WARNING SIGN.

"RECIPROCAL"...I LOVE TO SAY THE WORD. Most of us are aware of being in a state of reciprocity in our relationships. Did you know that this condition—or movement, if you will—has importance in math, genetics, foreign relations, insurance (!), surveying, electricity, and navigation? It's a big deal. And we all intuitively know it.

It means a mutual exchange, given or felt by each toward the other. It is a back-and-forth flow of energy that most of us like to have in some kind of balance. It may be verbal communication, nonverbal stuff, affection, money, shared secrets, eye contact, creative ideas—it can take many forms. In love, when we get a clue that we are giving more than the other, doing more than the other, we notice it and eventually begin to resent it. Not that we always have to exchange the same things or in exactly the same amounts, but it's usually got to be close.

I have heard spouses complain: "He never comes up with an original idea for an activity or an outing. I think of everything we do. I suggest picnics, movies, ball games...he comes up with nothing. I'm tired of it." Or: "I am so much more affectionate than she is." Or: "I just love him more than he loves me." Or: "I remember more occasions and give him more gifts than he gives me." Or: "I give her a lot more sexual attention than she gives me."

Reciprocity of energy, ideas, feelings, and behavior. Lack of it: early warning.

22. RECIPROCITY IN A RELATIONSHIP DEPENDS ON BOTH PERSONS RECEIVING AND ACKNOWLEDGING WHAT IS OFFERED.

WE MAY THINK THAT RECIPROCITY, or mutuality of exchange, is just two forces sending energy back and forth—a kind of "I'll blast you with my love, and then you blast me with yours." But real mutuality arrives when we are both capable of receiving and acknowledging what the other has to give. You can send your message to me all day long, and I can send mine right back at you, with the same intensity and content, but unless there is reception and acknowledgement, it's probably wasted. Just like other communications, my ability to receive your love and let you know that I know I am loved is critical. Think of it…if you're loving me for all you're worth, and I am just not getting it, how do you feel? Acknowledgement that you're getting something and that you value it is often more important than giving something back.

Reciprocity is not just trading a certain amount of love, tit for tat, as if love were pounds of flour or bottles of wine. True reciprocation involves receiving what the other has to give, no matter the amount or the description, and giving fully what you have to offer.

23. IT IS NOT YOUR JOB TO MEET YOUR PARTNER'S NEEDS.

I KNOW, IT MAY SOUND CALLOUS and unloving, but it's true.

The belief that it is your job to meet your partner's needs gets all too many relationships in deep trouble. "I am here to do what you need in order to be successful." Taken to the extreme, one person becomes a slave to the other.

This belief—that it is not your job to meet your partner's needs in an intimate relationship—does not mean that you can't or won't pay attention to what she needs and respond to that in some way. You may meet her needs completely by accident, just by being yourself. (Wouldn't that be grand?) If you believe that you are required to meet her needs (assuming you know what they are), you take away her responsibility and her power. You take away her chance to be a whole person in her own right. Your job is to be totally yourself and to take care of yourself, which can include paying attention to your partner and what she asks for.

You can listen, you can respond, you can serve, you can please, you can help, but you do not have the responsibility of meeting someone else's needs.

24. ONE THING FOLLOWS ANOTHER.

MOST OF US ONLY SEE THIS in hindsight. This is what the wise person, and the wise couple, sees in the present: that the choices made now will lead down a path and will set off a sequence of events.

This is easy to see in sex, how one look, one touch, one kiss leads to something else, which is followed by another something else. We've set something in motion that now has a course of its own.

This is why relationships are so hard to plan. Life is change. One thing happens, and it sets in motion something else, which in turn alters a course, and that changes, too. In a conversation, one offhand remark can change the whole process of the dialogue because it leads to something else. So it is with relationships. Looking back, you may see how one seemingly inconsequential choice led your life down a completely different road than you planned or thought possible.

We cannot change the fact that one thing follows another, but we can be aware of it and be flexible enough to make conscious choices along the way. When you say something or do something with another, it has consequences; it sets something in motion.

Be aware of your beginnings, of the words you say and the actions you take that may change another's life. Be conscious of what your intentions really are.

25. The more troubled the relationship with your parents, the more dependent you will be on your adult relationships.

A PERSON WHO HAS GROWN UP in a healthy household and who has a solid relationship with his parents will have a stronger sense of himself, feel more secure, and feel less dependent on an intimate relationship. With this background, a child grows to know and love himself. He is able to see himself as a strong, separate individual and reach a degree of emotional maturity.

By contrast, the child who grows up in a troubled or chaotic household, where volatility and drama are part of the daily fare, or in a house that is very tightly controlled, will learn to define himself in terms of the other person—his parent(s). This person—partially emotionally mature and basically reactive—will duplicate his reactionary, dependent stance in his marriage or partnership. It is not always a matter of insecurity fostering fear in later relationships (it does), but a broader picture of an adult identity being defined by the other. The partner's values, actions, words, wants, and needs take on a much greater significance than one's own.

In adulthood, these people take a dependent or counter-dependent stance. They either wait for, and depend on, others' actions, or they react in a rebellious or defiant way. People have varying responses to their own dependency, including resentment, anger, fear, and aspects of defensiveness.

Adult intimacy may have many of the same characteristics that a healthy relationship with our parents had. There is a balance of togetherness and separateness, safety and risk, freedom and limits, bonding and individuality. Too much of either sets the stage for trouble later on.

26. SUCCESSFUL RELATIONSHIPS HAVE FOUR COMMON THREADS RUNNING THROUGH THEM.

COMMITMENT, COMMUNICATIONS, ROLE FLEXIBILITY, and a strong sense of self are four vital characteristics for a successful relationship.

Interviews with long-term couples consistently reveal four important factors in maintaining a satisfying relationship. The first is commitment. Each individual feels—and conveys to the other—a sense of sticking with the process of the relationship as it changes. Commitment is widely misunderstood. It does not mean keeping the relationship the way it is, nor does it mean passively staying in the relationship without regard to quality. A loving commitment means staying engaged with your partner, resolving issues, managing conflict, and moving within the relationship as it evolves. Each party is committed to the process of the living relationship.

Openness in communications (see aphorism #2) is the blood of the relationship body and perhaps the most important of these four factors. Clean, self-responsible communications will carry a relationship through many changes. It is a pity we don't learn more about the fundamentals and the nuances of clear communications as young people; it would save a lot of relationships.

Role flexibility we probably think less about. This refers not just to the roles of provider and housekeeper, but emotional roles as well, such as nurturer, creator, listener, supporter, visionary, and critic...even masculine and feminine. I look at a role as an intersection of my wants and needs and another's wants and needs, the place where our intentions meet. Flexibility in your roles with each other means being able to be and act differently than usual or expected, to have different functions in your own life and with each other. Awareness of roles and flexibility are life giving.

The fourth thread is that each partner feels they have a separate identity, a sense of self that is strong and separate from their partner. When you feel your own sense of self, your own autonomy, it is so much easier to grant that to your partner and to accept his or her own separate path.

Commitment, communications, role flexibility, and a strong sense of self are four vital characteristics for a successful relationship.

(Thanks to Carl Rogers for first putting these concepts together.)

27. TO GET WHAT YOU WANT IN A RELATIONSHIP, YOU DO NOT HAVE TO DEFEAT WHAT YOU DON'T WANT.

THERE ARE VARIOUS STRATEGIES for getting what we want from our partners. First, we must accept and admit the idea that all of us, at some point, try to change our mates. I know, it's not 100 percent acceptance and love, but we do it anyway. We want to make them into what we want them to be. And, while we are all moving to that day of perfect love, there are various things we try along the way.

We reward the qualities and traits that are in line with our "ideal spouse" picture: praise, praise, kiss, kiss, applause, applause.

We attempt to wipe out the behaviors and traits that don't fit the picture. Point it out, cut it out, get that out of here.

We then may punish our mate for those behaviors and traits, if our initial attempts are not successful. "I don't like you." "No, you can't have any." "As a matter of fact, I'm thinking about leaving."

Following that, we may ignore, repress, or deny what we can't— or won't—accept. In order to avoid dealing with characteristics and behaviors that just will not fit our picture, we ignore them. But these characteristics, which we have tried so hard to root out of our partner's personality, have a way of turning up in one way or another…illness, passive-aggressiveness, blaming, and depression, to name a few.

We engage in these reward and punishment tactics in to have our mate meet our picture of the way it's supposed to be. So you see where the problem is. It's in the words "ideal" and "supposed to."

There is nothing in a relationship to defeat. Love is not interested in winning, changing, or punishing.

There is no victory in love, only continued movement to one's full potential.

28. WE WILL REPEAT WHAT IS INCOMPLETE.

IN GESTALT THERAPY, there is a particular way of describing an unresolved conflict or trauma from the past. You may draw a circle that is not quite complete, or you may hold your thumb and forefinger in an arc, just an inch or so apart. This is the unclosed circle that represents some important event or relationship in your life that has not been completed or resolved to your satisfaction.

These unclosed circles hold us back and keep us from being our whole, healthy selves, especially when those circles represent traumas with a family member or a first love. The job of the client and the therapist, in the present, is to revisit the relationship as authentically as possible and bring the client's feelings and beliefs about the relationship to some kind of closure. This allows one to leave the past in the past and move on.

Childhood abuse, abandonment, domination, illness, loss, a painful divorce, betrayal—all are examples of the pain we sometimes experience and sometimes do not do a very thorough job of dealing with. Some of the pain, resentment, fear, or anger is left over, in our minds, hearts, and bodies, and lingers as a residue that interferes with our present experiences and relationships.

Left unattended, this remains a challenge to our unconscious. Something healthy in us wants to have resolution, wants to have these feelings expressed, wants the circle closed. It is a part of our spirit, if you will, that wants to be fulfilled. And so we begin to work out these unresolved feelings in our present relationship.

Our wife becomes Mom. Husband becomes Dad. Present friends become childhood friends who hurt or abandoned us. Second wife becomes first wife. Our spouse becomes the authority figure we must rail against. All the while, we are working on an old relationship, an unclosed circle, trying to resolve it for ourselves.

We will continue to do this—continue to create relationships that give us the opportunity to work on these important issues—until we get it right. That is, until we get it right or give up and retreat to a position of safety and protection. This is not good for us or for the relationship. This leaves us behind our scars, passive and protected.

The needs that were unmet in our childhoods and the pain that was unresolved will be played out in our present intimate relationships until we face them and bring them to a close.

29. WE LIVE OUT OUR RELATIONSHIPS ACCORDING TO A MYTH.

ALL OF US HAVE A PERSONAL MYTHOLOGY. A myth is made up of symbols that are important to us, rituals we engage in, predominant themes in our lives, and stories that we carry about ourselves and others. Our own individual myth explains and, in some ways, guides our behavior. It gives meaning to our past, establishes a sense of continuity to our lives, and gives us direction for the future.

You have a central myth about yourself, a myth about your intimate relationships—including your family—and a myth about your children. These are all closely connected to your ideals, values, and the qualities in life you most admire.

An important function, or result, of this myth is how we go about choosing a mate and how we live out our intimate relationships. We all bring significant experiences with our opposite-sex parent, same-sex parent, siblings, and others close to us to our relationships. These experiences shape our myth and, in turn, shape our relationships. We could say that our myths about love and marriage, shaped by our past, are the screens through which our relationships must pass on their way to a home within.

A myth is not a lie, opposed to the truth. It is the story—multifaceted and complex—that we have formed to explain the truth. Some of it is conscious and can be openly talked about. Some of it is unconscious and just beyond our reach.

It is important for us to get acquainted with the story we think we are supposed to live out. It is important to know the ideals, values, hopes, and expectations we have of ourselves and of our mates. Most therapists accept the idea that we seek out and develop intimate relationships with those people we see as fitting into our personal myth, whether we are conscious of it or not. The more we know about that process in ourselves, the better our relationships will be.

30. ALL MESSAGES TO YOUR PARTNER CAN BE SEEN AS REQUESTS.

I'M SURE YOU HAVE DISCOVERED by now that communication is a complex business. The more we understand communications theory and our own style of sending and receiving messages, the better off we'll be in all of our relationships, especially our intimate ones.

This is just one piece of communications theory: every message you send to your partner contains a request of some sort. At the most abstract level, everything you say contains the content of what you say and also the message, "Listen to me," and probably, "Listen to me and validate what I'm saying."

We can see this easily when communication in a relationship breaks down and one party is offended because she hasn't been listened to — rather, she has been ignored. The content of the message she just sent then becomes irrelevant, and what becomes very relevant is her belief that she has not been listened to.

The request part of our message is very often not expressed in words and is sometimes difficult to detect. Often, we are afraid or embarrassed to say what we want or need directly, so we camouflage it or say it nonverbally.

"It's cold in here." (Would you turn up the heat?) "Aren't you cold?" (Would you turn up the heat?) "You know, I'm really chilly." She's smiling, eyebrows raised. (Would you turn up the heat?) "Don't you think we should keep the house at a higher temperature?" (Would you turn up the heat?) This example may or may not be amusing, but, believe me, the request part of the message is not funny when it's linked up with areas of the relationship that are emotionally loaded, conflicted, or tender in some way. When you're talking about past hurts, disagreements or — typically — sex, money, or spirituality, it becomes especially important to carefully express what it is you want and listen for the request from the other.

If the request is not stated directly and clearly, ask what it is, and find out what is wanted or expected of you.

31. RELATIONSHIPS THAT ENDURE ACCEPT SEPARATION AS A PART OF INTIMACY.

SEPARATION IS A TONIC FOR MANY AN ILL. It can provide drama and excitement. It can give partners a sense of themselves alone. It can help define boundaries between two people that need clarity and definition. It works to counteract that old demon, habit. And it can help in communicating well.

Wise couples stir in a little separation like salt in a soup. They realize that recharging one's own batteries alone gives one something new to bring back to the relationship. It can help you say, "This is me and this is my experience"—something that is always helpful in a relationship and especially useful in communications. Separation can help you feel more in charge of yourself and know the difference between you and your partner. In this way it helps counteract codependence, the act of leaning on each other too hard.

If you're bogged down in habit, locked in a moody struggle, bored with the routine—take a break. Ten minutes or ten days, you decide. Go get a sense of yourself alone again and bring it back to the relationship, shored up and ready for action.

As Kahlil Gibran says, "Let there be spaces in your togetherness."

32. Relationships are never static.

"THE LONG COURSE OF MARRIAGE is a long event of perpetual change, in which a man and a woman mutually build up their souls and make themselves whole. It is like rivers flowing on, through new country, always unknown" (D. H. Lawrence).

Even the relationships you see (or may be a part of) that look dead or strangled by habit and routine are changing, if for no other reasons than the individuals in them are aging and the world around them is changing. No matter how subtly, relationships are changing all the time.

Change happens from the inside as well as coming to us from our situation or context. We learn, we see the world differently, we want more or less, we gain something or lose it...and in so changing, our relationship changes. We change homes, change jobs, add to our family, lose someone, become ill, and become more enlightened. We're changed by natural events and things over which we have no control; we react and we change. We become more loving, or less. We see our partners and friends in a different way. We shift priorities and values.

The important thing about change is to realize that you and your relationship are going to be in a state of change forever—sometimes faster than you'd like, sometimes slower. Change is the constant, and it is how we respond to change that does a great deal in determining the quality of our lives.

The relationship that is flexible, adaptable, and open about the process of change will provide a healthy context for the individuals within it—and for other family members.

33. BROKEN TRUST IS THE DEATH KNELL FOR MOST RELATIONSHIPS.

THERE ARE TWO THINGS in the definite "killer category" for love and friendship: broken trust and loss of respect. Of the two, trust betrayed is the most dramatic and the most wounding.

I happen to think that respect is a vital part of a love relationship (see #84), and that loss of respect is a very important signal that the relationship is on its last legs. But this usually happens gradually, when we begin to realize that we don't value or admire the values and behavior of our significant other.

The breaking of trust hurts more and can throw us into a serious downward spiral. When the trust we hold for someone we love is betrayed, our sense of reality is shaken. What we thought was real suddenly is not. The ground we were standing on is unstable. "What is true anymore?" we ask ourselves. "What can we depend on?" "Who is that person across from me?"

Trust is tied directly to our security—one of our most important needs—and when our security is threatened, we pull way back into ourselves, shore up our defenses, and protect ourselves. For most couples, this nosedive is hard to pull out of.

Be careful with the trust another has bestowed on you.

34. BLAME IS A NO-WIN GAME.

HERE'S HOW BLAME WORKS: something goes "wrong." This is the first step toward blame: seeing events as wrong. When something goes "wrong," most of us start looking for cause and effect. Then we are ready to punish the perpetrator. This is the police-criminal way of looking at our lives. A crime is committed; we look for the criminal, blame the criminal, and punish him. Whether or not this works at a social level is questionable, but it does not work in intimate relationships.

Blaming usually leaves one partner feeling guilty, shamed, one-down, and/or rejected. It's hard to see how the partner doing the blaming could feel "good" about this, but some of us find reward in feeling one-up, dominant, righteous, or better-than. Righteousness, not a very attractive human trait, is probably what most of us get from doing the blaming.

This does not move us toward intimacy. It keeps a distance between the righteous and the guilty and maintains a balance of power, since the process of blaming is usually ongoing and not just a one-time event. It requires the participation of both parties because the blamed must agree to feel shamed, thus completing the punisher-victim circle.

For the most part, these are roles that are established early in the relationship. In terms of power, blaming aims to establish or perpetuate an imbalance, an inequality between two people, wherein one of the partners has the ability to see what is right and what is wrong. In an ironic way, blaming robs the blamer of power, too. When I blame you, I am saying that you—and only you—had the power to control what happened between us. There is a pushing off of responsibility in blaming. This is why I say that blaming comes out of a victim mentality: I blame others for what hurt me.

In the math of relationships, blaming is a zero-sum game for the relationship. Assuming we start out equal, if I blame you, the score is one-nothing in my favor. If you blame me, the score is one-nothing in your favor. This is just an ongoing win-lose battle, but the relationship gains nothing. The relationship gains when the score is one to one, when both of us win, or when there is no reference to winning or losing.

Blaming is an insidious and practically worthless process. Stepping out of blame means claiming your own full responsibility and power.

35. RELATIONSHIPS COME APART IN A FAIRLY PREDICTABLE PATTERN.

THE EXPERIENCE OF UNCOUPLING is very similar to coupling; you could almost just run the film backward. The process is subtle, at first. One of the parties initiates, just as in bonding, often without the full knowledge of the other, and the process gathers a momentum that is often difficult to stop. Uncoupling gradually moves from intimacy to alienation.

Usually, one party begins an emotional or psychological distancing long before their partner is aware of it. Sometimes the distancing occurs even before the initiator is fully aware. The initiator feels a lack of satisfaction or contentment and after awhile begins to express this. This is often done subtly or is ineffective, and the partner does not take full notice or discounts the complaints.

In a way, the couple is collaborating at this point to keep the real trouble of their relationship secret, either because they don't want to face the music and do the work, or because they are afraid. Each one may then choose something indirect and individual to compensate with—more work in their career, outside activities, intense self-improvement, or a lifestyle change—and in doing so, they slip farther away from one another. One or the other will usually have an outside confidant who will listen and support their point of view.

This is a danger point, and it is here that a confrontation usually occurs and the threat is more fully realized. During this stage, things are often said or done that damage the relationship even more and make reconciliation much more difficult. If there is a third party involved, especially a lover, the relationship often ruptures.

If the couple seeks help at this stage, they face the task of putting back together a relationship that has now been neglected for months (or longer) and taking care of hurts that have been festering and needs that have not been satisfied. For those of us who do couples counseling, it is our most frequent observation that couples come in too late, that they are closing the barn door after the cow has run off.

I am a big believer in preventive medicine for relationships. In this case, I mean that the relationship has been built on a foundation of trust, sensitivity, and open communications—the absence of which serve as early warning systems. When something changes and someone is not satisfied, that is immediately paid attention to.

This is not a guarantee that the parties will stay together in the same way, but it does represent the hope that they will each help the other to fulfill their destiny.

36. ALL RELATIONSHIPS HAVE CONFLICT; IT IS THE AMOUNT OF CONFLICT AND HOW YOU DEAL WITH IT THAT DETERMINES QUALITY.

I SEE CONFLICT AS A SYMPTOM. If we were all the same, had the same desires, loved each other the same amount, and saw the world the same way, we would not be in conflict. Luckily, that is not true. We are (vive le) different. Conflict is a symptom of differences.

Seeing conflict in this way allows you to change your attitude about conflict itself, which I believe is the most important step in improving the resolution of conflict. Once you change your attitude about conflict, you can approach differences between yourself and your partner with less of a "good" or "bad" label. You can see that you are simply different. Exploring those differences is a source of intimacy—maybe the most important source. Successful conflict resolution leads to intimacy.

If a relationship has no conflict, or the conflict is repeatedly suppressed, it is usually a flat or superficial relationship. If it has very little conflict, it is usually not very stimulating either. But if a relationship has too much conflict it can easily burn up the love between two people, draining most of the energy they have in the constant attention and work of resolution. In other words, a certain amount of difference between you and your partner is healthy and allows you to explore another's world. Too many differences present a big challenge that few are able to successfully deal with. And there are hundreds of ways we can be different.

Conflict is an ongoing part of life. It won't go away. It's a part of all relationships.

Unresolved conflict is one of the biggest weeds in love's garden, and two people with sophisticated skills in this department greatly increase their chances of staying together.

37. IF PHYSICAL LOVE IS TO BE MUTUALLY REWARDING, IT MUST BE FREELY GIVEN.

PHYSICAL LOVE, like emotional and spiritual love, involves a surrender of fear. Orgasm is an allowance: I am allowing my body and feelings to go through a natural and predictable process that has a buildup of tension and a letting go of tension. I allow this to happen. I give in to it. I surrender a certain amount of self-control. This cannot happen to its fullest extent, and perhaps not at all, if I am coerced, intimidated, manipulated, or afraid.

I may be afraid of myself, of what it will mean to me to surrender. I may be afraid of the consequences in the relationship. I may be afraid of not doing well, of performing poorly. I may be afraid of my partner's power, judgments, physical strength, or derision.

There are countless fears that hide in the vessel of sexuality. To many of us, sex is sacred, private, loaded with emotion, tied to other problems in our lives, and/or laced with anxiety.

For a true, whole union to take place, both partners must feel free and unafraid. Fear, as it does in the rest of our lives, thrives in darkness and secrecy. When fear is revealed, it turns out not to be as large and threatening as we thought. Honest communication with each other, and experiences that lead to trust, pave the way for a true union in sex.

38. SEX HAS MANY DIFFERENT REASONS AND FUNCTIONS.

JUST AS MARRIAGE IS MANY DIFFERENT INSTITUTIONS, sex happens for a variety of different reasons and serves many different functions, inside and outside of a marriage.

We have sex in order to reproduce, claim power, express anger, relieve stress, avoid conflict, make someone else happy, be held, feel close, dominate another, feed our egos, express love, have fun, become intimate, seduce someone into a relationship, keep a relationship together, satisfy a desire, or fulfill an obligation. I'm sure you can add to this list once you're in the spirit of it.

Often—maybe more often than not—we are having sex for a reason different than that of our partner.

The things that enable a satisfying sexual relationship for most people have to do with two things: the mutuality of these reasons and reciprocity. One, we are doing this with the same feelings and for the same reasons, and, two, on a more or less equal basis, what I give out comes back to me. It means that we are on the same page, and our energy is balanced. That can be within a very wide range of attitudes and behavior, but what matters is that the two of us agree on our own private sexual relationship.

I think the same thing is true about relationships in general: we can have any kind of relationship we want. What's important is that we both understand the rules and agreements and have a more or less equal amount of love exchanged. Lack of balance is what eventually spins most relationships out of control.

Sex is a highly loaded part of our love relationship, loaded with issues of security, ego, attachment, jealousy, envy, power, and love, to name a few. For that reason, sex is often an area of secrets and poor communication. Openness and clarity enhance the sexual act itself and add to intimacy in the relationship as a whole.

39. THE SEXUAL ACT IS A MICROCOSM OF THE WHOLE RELATIONSHIP.

THE PROCESS AND DYNAMICS of our relationship as played out in the bedroom can capture the satisfactions and disappointments of the way you relate to one another in general. Sex is a loaded, dynamic example of the way we relate.

Maybe by just asking a few questions, you'll see clearly what I mean. Imagine that there are two columns on a sheet of paper in front of you; one is headed "in bed," and the other "in the whole relationship." Down the left-hand side are these questions. Pencil ready?

Who initiates contact? Who is active, and who is passive? Who works to satisfy the other? Who is vocal, and who is silent? Who is afraid? Who takes risks? Who is more playful? Is one person overwhelmed or persuaded? Who is more in charge? Who is more tender? Who is satisfied first? What are the feelings afterwards? Who is more into it?

In this description, sex becomes a small mirror held up to the rest of the relationship in order to explore risk taking, power, personal contact, devotion, satisfaction, and the exchange of energy. This can be a useful process for looking at the process and satisfaction of your whole relationship.

40. A RELATIONSHIP WITHOUT FREEDOM OF CHOICE IS A RELATIONSHIP WITHOUT SPIRIT.

WITHIN ANY RELATIONSHIP YOU HAVE, choice is your fundamental right. Conscious choice is one of the most important gifts we human beings have, and when we are deprived of it, or think we are, we begin to lose our enthusiasm, our élan vital, and eventually our psychological health. We've all had the feeling of being trapped and remember how it affected us—no alternatives, no way out, no choices. It's deadening.

Choice first implies an awareness that we are in charge of our lives and can, in fact, choose. It also implies a range of alternatives to choose *from*, not an either-or choice between two alternatives we haven't generated. We are responsible for coming up with those alternatives.

It also means that we believe we can choose freely, that we don't feel pressured or coerced into one alternative. And it means that once we've chosen, we're responsible for our own choices and the consequences that follow. No excuses. No blame.

I think it's healthy to realize that you are choosing the relationship you're a part of on a daily basis. Every day you wake up, you're choosing to remain in that marriage, or work for that firm, or stay in that live-in relationship. It's empowering and life-giving to realize that.

Helping your partner to become aware of choices and to exercise them is an act of love.

41. THE MONSTER THAT EATS UP MANY RELATIONSHIPS IS HABIT.

HABIT IS NOT ALL BAD. Habit gives us some things that promote our health and safety. For the most part, we groom by habit: brushing, flossing, combing, and drying. We look before we cross the street. We shift gears. We buckle our seat belt. These are acts that we do regularly in the same way without a lot of thought and there are hundreds of these habitual acts that serve us well.

Habit also works against us. Intimate relationships are living, breathing organisms and they need movement and change in order to stay alive. They need a certain amount of unpredictability. Habit, in as much as it is largely involuntary and largely unconscious, can invade the parts of the relationship that thrive on life in the moment, choice, and conscious awareness. When these "supposed-to-be-lively" facets of your relationship are carried out by rote, intimacy is strangled.

What behavior is susceptible to habit? Almost anything you do. Thinking about intimate relationships, here are some things you might want to look at and, just for the hell of it, change the way you are doing it now, or where, or when: ways you say hello and goodbye, eating meals, having sex (including foreplay), drinking (alcohol), what you say or do when you awake, what you do when you first get home, what you call each other, what you wear (or don't), what you expect of your partner daily...and you think of something, too.

By doing something differently, you call attention to it. By calling attention to a habitual action, such as washing your hands, you give it a kind of life. Writers in Eastern philosophy write about dignifying the ordinary. We can do this by slowing down our pace, paying conscious attention and imbuing habitual, ordinary actions with attention and meaning.

42. DESIRE IS A STRENGTH AND A WEAKNESS.

I HAVE A SAYING: "It is good to be hungry when you know you can eat."

It feels good to want something when you can easily anticipate the fulfillment of that desire. But to be in a kind of permanent longing for something is a lousy place to be.

Western psychotherapists spend a lot of time urging clients to discover what they want, affirm what they want, and go after what they want. And Buddha writes that desire is the root of all our suffering. How do we reconcile these two positions?

It's more than just an intellectual dialectic, it is a daily experience. I want a house in the country, and I can't afford it. I want to be in a long-term intimate relationship, and I can't find it. I want you, and you don't want me. You want sex, and I don't. I want more communications in our relationship, and you don't. Sometimes our desire seems without limit and our conflicts unending. It can hurt to want and not have that want fulfilled.

On the other hand, if we did not want, that would seem to put an end to our motivation. How would we move toward goals? From where would our passion spring? Doesn't our sexual passion come from really wanting someone else? Isn't there a life lesson in that?

We want. We want what puts an end to our wanting. But we get what we want, and it doesn't end our wanting. We still want. Wanting is the issue, not the satisfaction of it. Wanting is a statement of not having. If I want, I don't have. If I have, I don't want. As the song says, "God bless the child that's got his own."

Recently I've thought that wanting is laced in tight with our ego. In the early part of life, we each need our ego strengthened. It is part of growing up, part of our development, and rightly so. It might even be said that the first 30 years or more of life are for strengthening the ego and meeting the wants and needs of the ego. We set goals, we acquire, we compete, we look good, we build families. We each answer the call of our ego and our desire.

Then perhaps we know when it is time to put ego aside. We realize that it is getting in the way of more important things...a deeper love, giving to others, serving society. Perhaps ego has blinded us from what we truly, deeply wanted. And desire, linked to our self-satisfaction, has kept us from deeply connecting to what we did have and what was closest to us.

Maybe the second half of our lives is a time for desire to be put away, like a coat that is too small for us now, so that we can be more truly present to the here and now, more intimate with the person in front of us, and more connected with a life flow that is already going on around us.

43. THE LOVER WHO IS THE OBJECT OF PASSIONATE DESIRE IS NOT FULLY SEEN.

THE NATURE OF PASSION is akin to fire. It consumes its object, and the object disappears. Passion, if it is the only basis for a relationship, is a weak foundation and susceptible to the winds of change and crisis. This is not to point out that passionate relationships are bad or good, but to see the results of basing a relationship *solely* on passion. It is helpful to see and understand the basis for your relationship and the ground on which you want to build. If you want some kind of constancy, stability, longevity, and depth, build your relationship on respect, acceptance, admiration, adoration, mutual nurturing, and tenderness. Passion requires a certain amount of imbalance, tension, and anxiety to exist.

Pepper Schwartz, in her book *Peer Marriage,* says this: "The early throes of passionate sexual attraction obliterate almost every other facet of the other person. The pure intensity of desire…is overpowering; lust overcomes all…. The lover in the clutches of desire is powerless for a time to resist the objectification of the other. The need, the desire is predominant."

Desire is not love. If you want something, you want it for yourself, for your own use. This, in itself, is not bad either. Some of us like it. But it is not love and should not be confused with love. True love wants *for* the beloved.

44. REJECTION IS RARELY A STATEMENT ABOUT THE ONE REJECTED.

REJECTED. Denied. Offered in the store window, looked over, handled, appraised, and left there alone. Not good enough. Not pretty enough. Not "together" enough. Not secure enough. Not enough.

It's hard not to take rejection personally. We usually take it to mean that we have failed, that we lack something or don't live up somehow. Being sent away usually cuts us to the quick, but we can look at rejection in another way. We will be much better off if we can see that rejection is much more of a statement about the person speaking or taking the action, than it is about the person being sent away.

Sometimes "rejection" is simply a matter of timing. One person in the relationship isn't ready for love or commitment, or one person realizes a growing apart before the other does. Timing is a very underrated factor in relationships—what he has just been through, what she is headed for, the relationship he just got out of, the balancing of priorities in her life—all of these may have to do with when you meet the other person in their life cycles. There is a time when a relationship will work and a time when it just isn't right. It's a mistake to take this personally.

Sometimes "rejection" is one partner seeing the nature of the relationship more clearly than the other and seeing that it really isn't working for either person. Pointing this out, which is often heard as rejection, may be simply telling the truth about the relationship.

And "rejection" is often a euphemism for, "I am just not loving enough right now." A person who sends a partner away is making a statement about their ability to love, their patience, their understanding, and, perhaps, their fear.

There is no guarantee against the end of a relationship. People change. Circumstances change. But choosing wisely in the beginning and keeping your eyes and ears open—while not guaranteeing anything—give you a much better chance of continuing a healthy relationship.

45. THE MANAGEMENT OF CONSENT GREATLY AFFECTS THE QUALITY OF ANY RELATIONSHIP.

THIS IS A VERY IMPORTANT PART of the play of power between two people, in organizations, and in society. The management of consent is a simple enough idea, but in practice, the failure to pay attention to it results in unresolved conflict, resentment, heel dragging, passive-aggressive behavior, and the waste of time and energy.

Simply put, managing your consent means that you alone are in charge of whether or not you fully participate in the ideas and initiatives originated by others...your partner, your supervisor, your congresswoman, and your cultural heroes. Just the phrase "managing consent" implies that someone is trying to get you to go along with them, and they are, every day. We are bombarded with appeals for our dollars, our votes, our time and energy, and our willingness to participate or behave in a certain way.

We are asked to consent because those in relationship with us—who want to exercise power—need us. A leader needs a follower, a teacher needs a student, a supervisor needs someone to supervise, and an artist needs a listener or a viewer in order to complete the loop, to make something meaningful happen.

Intimate partners need each other's consent in order to function well as a couple. Managing your consent in an intimate relationship is involved in almost everything you do together, from buying a house to having sex. It means you say yes when you fully mean yes, no when you mean no, and are willing to work out the feelings in between.

When you are the initiator of an action or an idea, take care to watch for the full consent of those you are asking to join you. Watch for the "false yes," or consent not fully given. Paying attention to this issue, and being able to work with it, greatly enhances the quality of any relationship.

46. Partners create an environment for one another.

A TEACHER CREATES AN ENVIRONMENT in a classroom. Leaders create an environment in their organizations. Physicians and psychotherapists create an environment in their offices. Some of this creation is conscious and deliberate, and some is not. Nevertheless, when we are in a family and in an intimate relationship, we take part in creating a psychological/emotional space for the other person(s) in that relationship.

I think it's important for you to focus on your role in creating spaces for those people you influence and to realize how these "personal environments" affect you.

Author and psychotherapist Carl Rogers, the founder of client-centered therapy, was very aware of this early in his career and virtually made it the cornerstone of his theories about relationships that heal. He contended that the therapist could consciously create a psychological greenhouse—an atmosphere based on acceptance, authenticity, and empathy—in which the client would thrive. Just as a plant does well under the ideal conditions, a person is encouraged to blossom when she recognizes that she is safe, in a real and honest relationship, and is deeply understood. The conditions of the relationship and the personal atmosphere created between the two people were more important to Rogers than most of the interventions the therapist made.

We all create mini-environments for the people we impact, those people close to us or somehow dependent on us: our children, employees, clients, partners, and even our parents. You might ask yourself some questions about the environments you are creating. Are they safe? Inviting? Tough? Warm? Accepting? Critical? Supportive? Judgmental? Angry? Loving? How would you like to change the climate you create?

When you consistently give another person attention, understanding, empathy, acceptance, and freedom to choose, she will return to the safety and closeness of the relationship over and over again.

47. LIFE IS LIVED IN RELATIONSHIP; RELATIONSHIP LIVES, AND DIES, ON TENSION.

WE CANNOT ESCAPE RELATIONSHIP. We begin our life in relationship. We live in relationship with our environment, plants, animals, and other people. When two or more people come together and want something with each other, something is born between them. The issue of power is raised; there is the opportunity to express power. This energy, or tension, holds the relationship up in a way, gives it vitality. If this tension did not exist, the relationship would collapse, as if air had been taken out of a balloon.

Life itself is based on this coming together of polarities. Sperm joins egg, cell joins cell, lover joins beloved, companies merge, we join with others to accomplish tasks...our life cycle is round after round of coming together—a buildup of tension and a resolution of tension.

That tension is based on differences. If we were all the same, there would be no life, literally and figuratively. The fact that we are different in so many ways is what makes us interested in each other and attracted to each other. This is what gives any intimate relationship the mystery and sense of discovery it needs to be lively.

These differences, or this tension, can be channeled into collaboration or into competition.

Couples come together to discover themselves in relationship and to do things in the world that they can't or don't want to do alone: bear children, build a home, build a family, start a business, find security, etc. This calls for a high degree of collaboration, and it is in these intimate relationships that we learn, by trial and error, and practice our relationship competency.

Basically, this collaboration means learning to accept and deal with differences. Too much similarity and the relationship may be flat. If there are too many differences, the relationship may be burned up by dealing with the constant conflict.

Tension is manifested in relationships as conflict or collaboration. Learn to balance and work with this tension from a place of inner peace.

48. ENTANGLEMENTS ARE NOT ENGAGEMENTS.

MANY MEN AND WOMEN are involved in relationships wherein boundaries are not clear, as if one country existed alongside another, but the citizens didn't know where the border was, where one country ended and the other began. We could call these relationships entangled, or enmeshed, and the partners generally do not have a sense of themselves as whole, independent persons on their own.

There are several important characteristics of entanglements. Usually they involve making an unconscious deal with the other person: e.g., you handle all the money and I'll take the lead socially; you think, and I'll feel; you don't talk about alcohol, and I won't talk about smoking; and so on.

These enmeshed relationships also exist by keeping certain secrets—certain areas of the relationship that are not up for discussion or change. These might involve sex, or no sex, excessive drinking, abuse, or other behaviors that are considered taboos. In addition, one partner is usually looking for the other to meet a set of expectations, without which they are not happy. So a certain amount of control, or attempt to control, is present.

Often, it is hard for one person to let the other completely feel their feelings. Emotions are strong and unpredictable, and as such, threaten to upset the carefully constructed structure designed to keep things in place. Conflict in general is very problematic in entangled relationships and is often suppressed, denied, or handled by trying to make the other person feel wrong.

Basically, in entangled relationships, you are trying to get something from the other person that you failed to get earlier in your life. You are looking to extract something from the other in order to complete yourself. You are probably threatened by their departure. Drama, threats, and manipulations are hallmarks of these kinds of relationships.

Entanglements do not have: spontaneity; the sense of one healthy, whole person engaging another; the freedom to approach, withdraw, and find a happy, flexible distance based on mutual feelings and responding easily to the needs of the present moment.

Entangled relationships, with their strictly enforced contracts, keep individuals locked in place. Loving relationships free the involved individuals to be who they are, without reference to deals made.

49. PARTNERS QUICKLY BEGIN TO MIRROR EACH OTHER.

PEOPLE WHO BECOME BONDED usually begin to imitate each other in ways that are both superficial and profound. Gestures, facial expressions, spoken phrases, and ways of dressing are consciously and unconsciously imitated. So, too, are ways of thinking, feelings, attitudes, and values.

Much of this similarity in our mates stems from our choice of partners in the first place. While we choose partners that are different and complement us, we don't make a choice that is too different; it feels like reaching too far. Many of our similarities, then, are born out of the culture that nourished us.

Beyond this, we can say that we mimic each other in some important ways. Very often, we develop a private communication system that only our partner can understand, complete with verbal and nonverbal codes. We begin to speak like they do, particularly if we admire them. Often we will use the same hand movement, smile, smirk, or look of disdain.

This is important to be aware of. Individuals who know each other well, who are connected with many "lines" between them, can take each other up or down the emotional ladder. Anger is mirrored with anger. Complaint echoes back as complaint. Negative thinking begets negative thinking. Pessimism can be contagious. Luckily, encouragement, nurturing, praise, respect, and love are mirrored as well.

50. SEEK A BALANCE OF VARIED RESOURCES RATHER THAN EQUALITY OF THE SAME THINGS.

TWO PEOPLE WHO SEE and acknowledge the different contributions made and resources held by their partner create a rich relationship. What brings balance and a healthy complexity to a relationship is not a "like-and-like" set of characteristics, qualities, or resources, but a complementary engagement of different kinds of contributions.

Equality and equity are not the same. I think the notion of equality gets a lot of men and women in trouble. In my way of thinking, equality is not so much to be strived for as is equity. Equality means alike in every respect, completely corresponding, of the same degree, value, or quantity. Equity means fair and just. Equal is more objective, equitable more subjective. Equal is easier to measure and to look at if we are seeking to blame. Equity means we are not exactly equal, but it feels right anyway.

Nature is not nearly so concerned with equality as it is with equity, with reaching a balance that keeps a system (or a relationship) whole and healthy. The enlightened couple will look more to natural law and recognize the place of many varied resources and characteristics, rather than trying to make each partner contribute the same.

FEAR

51. FEAR IS THE LOCKED GATE ON THE ROAD TO INTIMACY.

ALL OF US EXPERIENCE FEAR. All of us are, or have been, afraid to love. It is what we do with that fear that profoundly marks our loving relationships.

Our fear regarding relationships and love is learned. We were not born with our fears that have to do with intimacy. We learned our fears of lasting, whole love from our childhood experiences of inadequate or flawed love. The more flawed those experiences were, the greater our adult fear of a loving relationship.

Fear is a prediction. Fear is the process of taking an experience from the past and projecting it into the future. We cannot be afraid of anything unless we have experienced it at some level. Again, we were not born being afraid of loving or being loved.

A past full of pain and fear is carried with us and projected into the future of our current relationship. As that relationship becomes more intimate and we are more revealed, past fears rise to the surface of our psyches and take the form of avoidance, attack, defense, and conflict. This, we think, protects us by pushing away the other, who, in the language of fear, is the enemy. But this is the very person we have chosen to love and be loved by.

So, we seek to be in the state of loving and being loved, and, just as we are about to arrive, fear raises up its screaming, painful head and warns us away. Alarms go off. We are about to be hurt in the same way we were hurt in the past, and we must get out of danger.

This process, lived out over and over again, is the gate that stands in the way of you having what you want. You and only you have the key to dealing with your ability to love. You must learn about your own fear and become friends with it. Fear thrives in the darkness, in secrecy. Learn that you can bring it out, into your own full consciousness and the light of the relationship. Exposed, it will look different.

Fear is the single most important process that limits your love, destroys love between you and someone else, and curbs your capacity to be a loving human being.

52. OFTEN WHAT WE FEAR IS WHAT WE WANT THE MOST.

"HOW SHOULD WE BE ABLE to forget those ancient myths that are at the beginning of all peoples, the myths about dragons that at the last moment turn into princesses who are only waiting to see us once beautiful and brave. Perhaps everything terrible is in its deepest being something helpless that wants help from us" (Rilke).

Suppose all of our dragons are princesses in disguise? Think of the dragons you face in your own life, your deepest fears. Imagine them transformed, slowly changing to opportunities—invitations, even—to gain a new part of yourself, to learn, to absorb power that you have lost, to fill a void.

Fear is a prediction of the future based on past pain; it is nothing more than a prediction. Read that again and remember it.

What many of us need most of all is healing, and that healing is brought about by some kind of visitation, or encounter, with what hurt us. If we are to be truly whole, we must close the circles that have been left open in our lives. We must, in some way, revisit our pain. In this way, our lives will not be ruled by the fear of what once hurt us. We want this at a deep level. We want this in order to be healed. Some aspect of what we are afraid of holds a golden opportunity for growth and healing on our part.

What turns out to be most important are not the things of which we are afraid, but whether or not we live our lives laced with fear.

The worst has already happened to us, and now we live in fear of it happening again. Do not let fear rule your life.

53. THE FEAR OF LETTING GO HOLDS US BACK FROM CONNECTING DEEPLY.

ONE OF OUR STRONGEST, most prevalent fears is the fear of letting go. There is something about surrendering that is abhorrent to most of us, even if it is surrendering to an urge in ourselves. Control is a safer place to be.

We must let go of some things in order to move on to others; we must shed an old skin in order to live in our new one. This is part of developing into our full potential. The same is true of relationships. The relationship must change and move on to a new phase or it faces a rigid stagnation.

If we refuse to let go and allow ourselves to move on, to learn something new about the unknown and ourselves, the relationship suffers. We stay at (or move to) a superficial level and fail to deeply connect, or we fail to stay in contact with a partner who is learning and growing.

The fear of letting go is very apparent in sex. Are you able to surrender to your own urges and those of your partner? Does your body completely let go? Or does some part of you observe, hold back, and attempt to control what happens? To be able to surrender and completely let go, to lose control in the safety of another's embrace, is one of the reasons we have sex. It's what makes sex transcendent. You can learn a lot about your fears by exploring this part of your life.

This fear of letting go is a tricky fear; you say to yourself, from that place of fear: "What if I totally let go and act out all that I am, give all of myself, and still come up short? What will I have left? Nothing!" So we hold back. We control. We become comfortable in the relationship, and it begins to become habitual.

Living things grow. A relationship is a living thing, and it thrives when the individuals in it are not bound or stagnant. Relationships, in order to stay alive, require the ongoing surrender of things you want to hold on to. When you feel safe, you'll be able to let go. If you don't feel safe, pay attention to your fears and resolve them. You are worth the effort.

54. ALL OF US ARE AFRAID.

ISN'T IT ODD? We run around thinking how unique we are and how uniquely large our fears are, and when we bring them out, we see that all of us loving human beings are afraid and are often afraid of the same things. All of us.

We can categorize our fears, talk about them a little, and whittle them down to a size that can be managed. Fear thrives in the darkness, when it is unexposed. I strongly recommend talking about your fears as a way of deepening your intimacy.

Fear has many faces, but there are some more basic fears we have in intimate relationships. We are afraid of: being overwhelmed, being abandoned, letting go, being exposed, being attacked, and hurting the ones we love.

The fear of being overwhelmed is the belief that you and I will merge and I will lose my own identity. If I give myself to you completely, I will disappear and lose myself to your control. I learn this from dominating parents.

The fear of being abandoned is in the belief that I will eventually lose you and be alone, without defenses. Loss and helplessness will fill my life after you walk away from me, which I know you will do. By myself, I fear, I am no one. I learn this from being left alone without sufficient attention.

The fear of letting go stems from a lack of trust of my own psyche or my own body. I am afraid that if I surrender and lose control, I will hurt myself, be hurt, or hurt others. The fear of letting go may mean a lack of experience or may be based in a life full of criticism for my behaviors.

The fear of being exposed stems from having something to hide. Intimacy will bring the discovery of my secret flaws, my ugly side, and all my faults. Rejection will surely follow that discovery, for I believe I am unlovable. I learn this from continually being judged and criticized.

The fear of attack is rooted in the belief that my partner will soon become dissatisfied, frustrated, and angry with me because my way of loving cannot meet her needs. Emotional and possible physical abuse will follow, leaving me wounded and forlorn. I learn this from unhappy, angry parents.

The fear of my own destructive impulses means that I believe I will eventually bring pain, unhappiness and even death to the one I love. I always hurt the one I love. Don't get close to me; I'll destroy you. I learn this from an alienated and violent past.

After reading these and feeling thoroughly depressed, read the previous aphorisms on fear again. Fear is a prediction based on the past. Let go of the past. Write yourself a new story. Discover that your fear is learned and can be unlearned. Discover that fear points toward personal growth.

POWER

55. RELATIONSHIPS ARE AS MUCH ABOUT POWER AS THEY ARE ABOUT LOVE.

YOU HAVE TO CLEAR YOUR HEAD about power to fully accept this one. If you think power means domination, control, and manipulation, you will misunderstand this. Some relationships are fraught with domination, control, and manipulation, but not the healthy ones. Strongly bonded intimate relationships are made up of individuals who are comfortable with their own power and that of others.

I define power as the capacity to experience yourself, coupled with the abilities to respond to that experience effectively. Healthy power is a means, not an end—a process, not a goal. The depth of your own power depends on how you experience yourself—your beliefs, your ideas, opinions, observations, feelings, wants, and needs—followed by how you act on those. Power has two faces: capacity and action.

In an intimate relationship, two people work out a balance of power that affects many issues: money, sexual behavior, child rearing, religious practices, decisions about everyday life, use and choice of food, care of the home, choice of clothes...literally everything they do together. Who decides? Who chooses? How is the decision made? How are they to live, and where? All of our life choices in a relationship involve the use and balance of power.

In a couple, it is important for each individual to realize their own power and for them to be able to act in concert, in order to be powerful together. How they experience themselves as a couple and how they act to manifest that experience and reach their goals is vitally important.

Further, it's important to realize that the expression of power is a necessary part of loving. We all have power and can use it to loving ends. I can use my power to manipulate you, or I can use it to nurture you and join with you. The fact that I feel deeply and express it to you in many ways is an expression of my power. As Martin Buber said, "We cannot avoid using power, so let us love powerfully."

The more powerful you are, the more you will be able to love. When two powerful people come together, they can create a powerful relationship, marked by a full expression of who they are as individuals. Learn as much as you can about your own power, and you will be more able to express your love.

56. THE BALANCE OF POWER IN A RELATIONSHIP IS DETERMINED EARLY AND GENERALLY STAYS INTACT.

THE BALANCE OF POWER in a relationship is worked out in many, many ways, some direct and some sneaky. I believe that men and women who are in the early stages of an intimate relationship experiment with power in the first minutes, hours, and days and eventually work out a power balance that sets the tone for the rest of their relationship. Sometimes, the way their power is exercised with each other proves more important than the love they have for each other. This does not necessarily mean that it's a detriment to their relationship. Couples who have their power issues worked out early may experience a freedom from conflict and a harmony that others lack.

We have different ways of being powerful. Some people are imaginative. Some are decision makers. Some prefer logic. Some depend on intuition. Some dwell in feelings and others in observation and research. Some are strong with words and others with their actions. And we are powerful in different areas of our lives: finance, food, care of children, mechanical things, medical care, sexuality, organization, and so on.

Smart couples explore their strengths and weaknesses, work to improve their weaknesses, and are able to accept and use resources in themselves that vary. They become a strong team because they complement each other and don't resent their differences.

However, a severe imbalance of power in a relationship is problematic. The ship that lists too far in one direction can't sail smoothly, especially through rough waters. One is too dependent on the other. One leans too far. Gradually the bond is weakened, or strength—and weakness—is resented.

All health depends on balance and so do relationships. Balancing the exercise of power is a critical element of long-term intimacy.

57. We Attempt to Gain Power in a Relationship by Defining Reality.

ONE OF OUR FIRST ACTS in any relationship is to try to find out what is real. "What's happenin'?" "What's going on here?" "What's the situation?" "What do we have here?" Language from the streets, the military, law enforcement, and the emergency room illustrate and reinforce this. We are trying to find out what the reality is in a given moment, so we can act accordingly.

We do the same thing in courtship. We try to separate illusion and fantasy from what is really going on with our partner. How do they really feel? What are they really like as a person? What is this relationship really like?

Once we find this out to our satisfaction, we not only begin to operate on it, but we try to convince others it is the truth. "This is the way things are," we say. We are attempting the same thing when we say, "You know what your problem is?" or, "The problem with our marriage is…" or, "The fact is, we can't afford a new car." We are attempting to define reality—and not just our own, but the reality on which we both now need to operate.

Initially, we discover what is real from our direct sensory experience. Later, we find out a lot of what is real from our parents; they tell us what is true about relationships, power, morality, love, reward, punishment, and marriage. This learning goes well until we discover that we are denying our own reality and accepting that of someone else. This is an important change and part of becoming a healthy adult. The building of your own power base begins when you define what is real for yourself and act on it, when you are able to trust your own core experience.

I can establish power in relationship with you by defining reality. I do this by telling you "The Truth" about the relationship, defining what is possible and what is not, by setting standards, imposing values, making moral judgments, and controlling reward and punishment. Sound like parenthood? That's what we learn to do, and that's what we carry over into our intimate relationships.

Optimal relationships are defined, in part, by individuals who have an equal say in defining reality and how it changes.

58. IT IS ONE OF OUR DEEPEST HUNGERS TO BE SIGNIFICANT.

ANOTHER WAY OF SAYING THIS: it is one of our deepest fears that we will be insignificant, especially to the one we love. There are a lot of ways to let a person know they mean little or nothing to you: not listening, not hearing, discounting their point of view, ignoring their feelings, not acknowledging their wisdom...anything that says, directly or indirectly, "Your voice, your person, does not matter." Even not looking at a person, when either of you is speaking, may be a way of commenting on their significance, or lack of it.

We all hunger for attention. We all want to mean something important to someone else, or lots of someones. It is the deepest kind of statement a human can make: "I mean something; I matter."

We may mean something to ourselves, but for nearly all of us, that is not enough. We want to make a difference in the life of another, and that gives our life meaning.

59. INCLUDING YOUR PARTNER HELPS HER FEEL SIGNIFICANT.

TO HAVE THE FEELING that we are significant is not about gaining fame or having a false sense of importance, but feeling that someone finds us valuable and meaningful. To feel significant is to feel that who you are is somehow vital and valuable to someone else; we are seen and recognized as important.

The opposite of feeling significant is to be invisible, disregarded, unimportant, and without meaning. It's a horrible thing when children or adults have this feeling about themselves.

Now, I don't believe it is one person's responsibility to cause another to feel significant, but we certainly can help, and in doing so, we can round out the responsibility in the relationship and add to its richness.

Feeling significant is one aspect of feeling our own power. It's a feeling state that results from communicating who we are with others and having that communication received and valued by them. We can help ourselves feel significant by exercising our full power, by being and saying who we are and taking responsibility for it.

We can help others feel significant by including them, by listening to what they have to say, and by being attentive to their wants and needs. We can seek out their opinions and feelings, we can bring them in on planning, and we can include them in our own inner processes, as we come to decisions that affect us and/or them.

We all want to feel significant. Significance follows inclusion.

60. YOU CAN RENDER YOUR PARTNER POWERLESS BY NOT ALLOWING HER TO IMPACT YOU.

WE ALL KNOW THE RESPONSE...or lack of it—the grunt, the lack of eye contact, the unfeeling, "Yeah, sure," the dull look in the eyes—all signs that you are having little or no impact. This lack of response is symbolic of not having power or significance with another. This way of responding is something you can control.

The artist, the entertainer, and the comedian are all in touch with this exchange. They know that the audience has a great deal of power in their relationship...the power of responding with enthusiasm and emotion or sitting on their hands and doing nothing. When you respond to someone, you make that event a synergetic experience, instead of just one person or one side "playing" to another.

One of the ways we can look at power is to say that it's representing yourself in the space of another person and having that representation mean something or have impact. When we talk to others, we watch carefully to see how it impacts them, to see if it moves them in any way. We especially do this when what we have to say is very meaningful to us, or secretive, or makes us feel vulnerable, and/or we believe it to be important to the other. So we watch to see how our message affects the other.

If we see little or no impact, at least two important things can happen: we lose interest, and/or we feel powerless. The easiest example is child to parent, although it is just as true in adult-to-adult relationships. If a child continually sees that his mother is not listening or not being changed in some way by what he is saying, he eventually believes that he has no power. These early relationships in the family are the training ground. We repeat our learning in our adult relationships.

Conversely, by allowing your partner to impact you, you tell them that they are important—that they are significant to you and that they are powerful. Since it is one of our deepest hungers to be significant, if we repeatedly see that we are not, we will go away and hide or find someone with whom we can be significant.

We all want to have an impact on another, and sometimes you can "steal" another's power by being indifferent.

61. WE MAY SUPPORT EQUALITY AND POWER IN OUR PARTNERS... UNTIL IT THREATENS OUR OWN.

IT IS EASY TO TALK about becoming equal and empowering others, but it is often another matter when it is time to act on it...when push comes to shove, as they say. Generally, those people holding the most power in a relationship will be reluctant to accept or allow true equality *if* they see it as a process of giving up some of their own power.

If you come from the belief that power is to be sought after and held for its own sake, you will subtly but surely discourage and suppress a partner because you think you will lose your own power. This is a misunderstanding of power; this view is more about control.

Encouraging personal power in another and taking actions that promote equality are two of the mains tasks of intimate relationships. While another's growth is not your responsibility, there are things you can do to help empower another. Giving up your own power is not one of those things. I do not suggest, either in a marriage or in a corporate hierarchy, that one person give up power in order to make another more equal. That is a lose-lose in my book.

The person with more perceived power in the relationship could use his or her power to include, to reveal, to nurture, and to encourage, rather than to compete or attempt to control. It is also helpful to realize and discuss that different people, and different genders, are powerful in differing ways.

In the end, it is up to each one of us to exercise our own power and not depend on anyone to give it to us.

62. FACED WITH POWERLESSNESS IN OUR RELATIONSHIP, WE MAY PREFER TO CLING TO OUR ILLUSIONS.

ALL OF US DELUDE OURSELVES about our closest relationships. We fool ourselves, or see things the way we want to see them, in order the preserve the relationship and our own point of view.

A common, if not pervasive, example is about "being faithful." We much prefer to see our partner as faithful only to us, and so we maintain that view, even if evidence is presented to the contrary. To see or admit something else would be to shatter the basis of the relationship and throw us into a situation we could not (so we believe) tolerate.

Our sense of power is an important factor in maintaining any illusion. When we feel strong, secure, and responsible for ourselves, and in touch with our own power, we are much more open to seeing the truth of our relationship and who our partner really is. At the other end of the spectrum, in our weakness, insecurity, and lack of resources, we will hold on to illusions because they prop up our lives.

This is the house of cards that comes tumbling down when an affair is discovered or when money troubles surface that were previously hidden. Our illusions are suddenly shattered, and we feel hurt, betrayed, and angry.

Perhaps we have refused to open ourselves and see the truth.

63. LOVE IS PRECEDED BY POWER.

TWO FUNDAMENTAL HUMAN TRAITS emerge as we grow and experience our lives: to be able (power) and to relate in a bonded, benevolent way (love). Power and love are two of our most fundamental reasons for being and we cannot fully love unless we are powerful.

At an early age, we learn how to behave in order to bring about change; we learn to respect our own experience and communicate to get what we want. These are our early lessons about power. We also learn how to relate to others, to care for ourselves and others, to feel bonded and compassionate…the beginnings of love. Too many relationships are profoundly unsatisfying because one or both of the partners are deficient in their ability to care for themselves and, as a result, lean too hard on the other person. They have learned too little about their own power.

Until you learn that you are responsible for yourself, that you can have an impact on others and they can have an impact on you, you will not learn to relate in an intimate way. You will not learn to love without the experience of your own power. To the degree that you feel able to affect and be affected, you will be able to give and receive love.

We need power (the capacity to experience ourselves and respond effectively to that experience) in order to affirm and assert ourselves, in order to form relationships. We form relationships to meet our needs, to love and receive love. In a real sense, we arrive at love through power.

64. LOVE IS POWER MADE VISIBLE.

MOST OF US SEPARATE LOVE AND POWER, elevating the former and eschewing or demeaning the latter. Love is good. Power is undesirable, we think, especially in a love relationship. We speak as if love cannot be abused. This is an illusion that only encourages powerlessness and eats away at our love.

Power and love are not mutually exclusive. In fact, both are fundamental to our human experience and work together as two hands cooperate to form a clay vessel on a wheel. We cannot have love without power.

We cannot have love unless we can experience our own selves, unless we can express ourselves, unless we have something to give, unless we can receive with grace, unless we can make ourselves significant in some way.

Think of some of the things you consider "un-love": fear, anger, punishment, abuse, alienation, and violence. These are behaviors of the weak, defensive, and alienated. These are things brought on by a sense of powerlessness. Think of love and violence as polar opposites, love being an expression of enabling and empowering, while violence is an expression of the frustration of wanting to control and not being able to. Think about power and powerlessness.

Love is an end to which we can use our power. Love is power made visible.

65. POWERLESSNESS IN A RELATIONSHIP FOSTERS THE ACCEPTANCE OF UNHEALTHY CONDITIONS.

WHEN A PERSON DENIES HER OWN POWER and allows herself to be dominated, it not only renders the partnership ineffective, it encourages the tolerance of conditions and behaviors that can be harmful or unhealthy. Put another way, if you are feeling powerless in a relationship you will tolerate things you would not normally accept.

Powerless might mean being out of touch with what you want or need, being ineffective in bringing about change, lacking communications skills, feeling afraid, shutting down...all of these mean you are not functioning optimally. As a result, you will tolerate emotional or physical abuse, a relationship that doesn't meet your needs, dominance by your partner, and/or the denial of your feelings and desires.

A good example of this principle might be found in a relationship between management and labor. If the workers in a plant are without a power base of any kind, they will tolerate a poor environment, low wages, long hours, and other unsatisfactory working conditions. Once a power base is established by employees—a strong union or a cooperative labor agreement, for example—they will no longer tolerate the unhealthy conditions. They have a power base from which to ask for what they want.

The same holds true in an intimate relationship. As long as you are in a one-down position and believe you are without a power base, you will tolerate some of the same things...a poor environment, low rewards, long hours, and an unsatisfactory relationship.

The antidote: find your way back to your own core experience, trust it, believe what you observe, think, feel, want, and need, and find the courage to act on that experience.

66. TREATING ANOTHER BADLY IS OFTEN A SIGN OF YOUR OWN POWERLESSNESS.

IF YOU ARE DEFICIENT IN SOME WAY—not whole, not optimal, not satisfied—it is very easy to turn on someone close to you and subject them to your blame, judgment, aggression, or violence.

If you are not doing what you want, fulfilling your needs, or acting out of your best, loving self, you are deficient. You lack something important. You are not acting out the best, optimal, powerful you. It may be hard to admit, but you are temporarily incomplete.

There is no one to blame for this. You are an adult and are responsible for meeting your own needs. No one else is responsible. But often you deny your own responsibility and power and lash out at others for not being who they are "supposed" to be, or doing what they are "supposed" to do for you. This is a denial of your own responsibility. It is also a signal that you need to pay closer attention to taking care of yourself, getting your needs and wants met, and increasing your capacity to love.

Powerlessness leads to dissatisfaction, which leads to dumping your stuff on someone else. Cut it out. Take control of your life, and use your power to love.

MARRIAGE

67. MARRIAGE HAS MANY DIFFERENT FACES.

MARRIAGE IS A RELATIONSHIP with many different facets and scores of variations. Though it is largely defined by the culture in which we live, our individual choice and various urges give the institution of marriage endless variety. Most of us enter into marriage romantically; this is one of the faces of marriage. It is a romantic relationship, at least for most of us and, at least, in the beginning.

It is also a legal agreement. It is often a religious relationship. It is financial. It is social and tied to other social institutions, such as churches, banks, schools, other families, and so on. It is a sexual relationship. It is cultural and national, that is, tied to formal and informal laws that are part of our nation and not necessarily part of others. It is also a psychological relationship, unconsciously designed for us to challenge ourselves and work out individual issues.

Another way of saying this is that people get married for many different reasons. Some marry for money, for love, for citizenship, for security, for regular sex, to gain the sanction of the church, to raise a family, to have an identity, to conform, to do the right thing, to be accepted, to move to a new social class, to leave the country and escape home and family.

Just as the word "love" means many things to many people, marriage is a many splendored thing (or a many splintered thing). It has numerous facets, and it will serve you well to examine them all and talk about them before you say, "I do."

68. OUR IDEAL MARRIAGE IS NOT OUR REAL MARRIAGE.

THE UNIVERSE IS MADE UP of things that join. Marriage is our most familiar response to our own urge to join. We are putting together polarities, just like the rest of nature. In putting together our own life with someone else's, we are inevitably faced with the myth of the perfect marriage or the idea of absolute harmony between partners.

Nearly every couple tries to achieve this perfect harmony, and if they do not, they still try to give their friends, family, and children the appearance of the perfect marriage. Even if the effort to convince others fails, they still tend to judge the relationship against the standards of the perfect marriage. This is substituting fiction for the truth.

The reality of marriage is not just one reality. There is no one real, perfect marriage. The reality—and the joy—is whatever happens to individuals in each marriage. The reality is your own experience. Awareness of that experience, awareness of your patterns and reflexes, leads to freedom from the ideal.

The ideal marriage, while a very strong part of our imagination, is not an achievable goal and not even a goal worth pursuing. Serve yourself by making the relationship you are a part of as healthy and as loving as it can be. Forget "perfect."

69. MARRIAGE IS NOT A GUARANTEE OF LOVE OR ANYTHING ELSE.

IT'S SAFE TO SAY that about half the population has had a painfully negative experience with marriage. Yet we keep on trying. After all, we do have an "urge to merge," and we do want some social stability around relationships, and we do want a stable form in which to raise our children. These are the benefits of marriage, to a society and to individuals.

What does this have to do with love? Love, I think you would agree, is the strongest and deepest element in all our lives, and we spend much of our lives looking for it, negotiating around it, and dealing with it when it is over. It is the companion of hope, of joy, of ecstasy. Love is meant to nurture us and, in its purest form, to set us free. Sometimes we try to equate love with marriage, in spite of the evidence.

To expect that marriage be "required" to hold perfect love for the length of a life or even the length of a marriage is a very high expectation, and not everyone will achieve it. In our social institutions, we have set up standards and expectations that are exceedingly high and lead to a lot of disappointment.

The promise of mutually exclusive love that lasts forever is a promise that, most of the time, is not kept. Yet, we persist in preserving that fiction, and we even make it a requirement in the minds and hearts of those of us who march to the altar. Looked at from afar, it must seem like a grand hypocrisy or a cosmic joke.

The point is, we have terribly high expectations of marriage and think it's going to guarantee love as long as we're married. You and I might love each other for as long as we're married. We might not. I don't see this as a reason to stop being a couple, but we might want to change our vision, our pledges and our "rules" about marriage. And about divorce.

What hurts most of us are our expectations and illusions about the institutions of marriage and family. Our continuing "romance" about those two things perpetuates those illusions. I'd like to see us all get more realistic about marriage. I'd like to see us help young people learn what marriage really is and what it is not. Why don't we truly educate ourselves about an institution that, when it fails, costs us so much?

70. FORMING INTIMATE RELATIONSHIPS IS BASED IN OUR CULTURE.

"MORE THAN OUR BIOLOGY?" you ask. When it comes to the issues that trouble us most: yes, yes, yes. Marriage and other relationships, as well as the rituals woven through them, are based in our society's values, norms, and mores. One need only leave the culture for a while and become acquainted with relationships in very different cultures— Africa, China, India—to see this more deeply.

What's equally important is that our attitudes leading up to forming relationships are programmed by our culture: what we think of ourselves if we are not in relationship, what we expect of ourselves when we meet the mate of our dreams, the expectations and illusions we have about the institution of marriage itself. All of these are culturally learned and reinforced.

Okay, okay, this is fine academically and all that, but what does it mean to us as individuals, and in plain language?

Our culture tells us how to be married. The lessons we have learned—from our parents, television, movies, books, teachers, and friends—all combine to tell us what married partners are and how they relate to each other. So we do it. Then one day, some of us wake up and say, "What the hell have I been doing? I don't want this kind of relationship. I've been duped."

Many people have seen that culturally enforced norms are not good for them, and they want to change them…at work, at home, in their relationships, and in the image they have of themselves and others.

Just remember that when you get married, you are engaging in a culturally sponsored event and that the expectations and norms surrounding that event are largely a product of your culture. Be aware of that. Retain your own choice and flexibility, and you'll be a happier camper.

71. WE THINK OF MARRIAGE AS AN END; SUBCONSCIOUSLY WE HOLD IT AS A MEANS.

WE CONSIDER, FOR THE MOST PART, marriage as a point of arrival: "There, we've done that; that's over with; now, we can settle down." We have gone through dating, courtship, and our engagement and found our lifelong mate. The battles are over. The war is won. We can relax and pay attention to our career(s) and building a home and family.

This is an illusion, as anyone who has been married for years can tell you. The forming of a significant, intimate relationship is a very important point of departure. As we grow closer and become more known to another, our deeper personal issues are raised, our fears come to the surface, and our attitudes about conflict and learning about ourselves come into perspective. Our spirituality becomes more significant. We begin to learn what it really means to love another. And we learn how we really feel about ourselves. All this is brought about in relationship, and that, in a way, is the "job" of relationships.

Our intimate relationships are means for self-knowledge, mutual satisfaction of needs, and living out our deepest loving selves, among other more conventional reasons.

Marriage is definitely "on the way" and not a final destination.

72. WE MARRY OUT OF FEAR AS WELL AS DESIRE AND LOVE.

ONE PARTNER MIGHT SAY TO THE OTHER: "It is not an accident that I chose you. I chose you to resolve something. I saw in you something that I wanted to have. I saw in you someone I could love. I saw someone who could love me.

"And, I have to admit now, I saw something that I feared and did not trust. I believe you saw this, too, but we did not talk about it. I was afraid that you would not love me, especially if you knew how little I loved myself, how worthless I felt, how controlling I was. I could not reveal these things to you. The risk was too great.

"The curious thing is, I found myself trying to induce feelings in you of rejection, of anger—almost asking you to push me away. I did this because it would prove what I secretly feared; it would fulfill this secret prophecy of mine that you would leave me if you really knew me.

"I see that we married in order to deal with our self-esteem issues. You seemed to value me, and I said to myself that I was lucky to have someone who cared for me. I see that you made me feel complete in a way that I didn't on my own.

"I think we both agreed to do this at an unconscious level. We agreed to live for each other, to form this survival pact that was somehow against the rest of the world. I knew if I ran out of the will to live, I could take from you. This worked for a while.

"When the stresses and challenges that affect all marriages began to impinge on us, it all kind of cracked. We began to see the 'ugly' side of each other, the side we had hidden so well in our courtship and early marriage. I see now that there is not a real ugly side, just a human side, a weakness that we both had but kept from one another. But when it all poured out, it was so unexpected and too much for either of us to handle.

"I put you in charge of my self-esteem. How could I ever expect that of anyone? I believed I had to please you, always. If I didn't, I couldn't stand your disappointment or anger. I guess, in the end, I married to get something from you that I never really had: my acceptance and love of myself."

Wouldn't it be marvelous if we knew all this and could talk openly about it in the beginning?

73. THERE IS NO "GOOD WIFE" OR "GOOD HUSBAND," ONLY THE PERSON YOU ARE HAPPY LIVING WITH.

OH, I KNOW THERE ARE PEOPLE about whom you just want to say: "He'd make such a good husband" or, "Mary, you're gonna make someone a damn fine wife." It does say something, but I also find it limiting, and I know many people who would take it as an insult.

A more important aspect of this is the energy we spend trying to become a good wife or a good husband, in the generic sense and without reference to a specific mate. Like "the good marriage," we hold a picture in our minds of what it's supposed to be, and we are often disappointed when we discover that our picture or prediction is a long way from reality. Our ideas of what marriages are supposed to be and what good spouses are supposed to be lead to a lot of divorces.

There are many, many kinds of marriages and many, many forms of intimate relationships that are satisfying to the people involved. Some of those look traditional, like the "nuclear family," but most are not. The best judges of what makes up a good relationship are the people involved. Even the educated eye sometimes finds it difficult to discover what moves two people to come together and remain coupled.

Rather than trying to become "a good wife" or "a good husband," put your energy into becoming who you want to be: an authentic, caring, responsible person who wants to love and be loved. Maybe you'll find another one.

LOVE AND INTIMACY

74. IT IS AN INHERENT PART OF OUR NATURE TO BOND WITH SOMEONE(S).

WE ARE NOT BORN ALONE, and we are not meant to live alone. Humans are social, loving animals by nature. Even the most isolated or alienated individuals among us want, at some level, to know and be known, to love and be loved. It is our destiny to form close, meaningful relationships.

Fear, accumulated emotional pain (fear), and lack of openness (fear) keep us from realizing our original and inherent nature: trusting, being open, and loving. It is a very important and hopeful piece of information that we are born wanting to bond, and that we subsequently learn to be afraid. Once we realize this and admit it to ourselves, we can make a commitment to moving more in the direction of love. When we realize we have learned our most important fears, we can make a commitment to unlearn them. Easier said than done, but worth it, very worth it.

75. WE DON'T KNOW WHAT LOVE IS.

YEAH, IT'S JUST LIKE THE OLD SONG SAYS. The fact is that many of us wouldn't know love if it walked up, shook our hand, and introduced itself. We think we know. We say we know. But we don't.

We all know that "love" is one of those words that we use a lot. We use it in many different ways, and it means different things to different people. Yet we go on believing we know what it means and believing we agree on it.

"I love your new sofa." "I love my dog."

"My mother loves me." "Don't you just love the smell of lilacs?" "God, I love those Knicks." "I love you, and I always will." We each grow up with a different meaning of the word love, of what it means to give, to receive, to nurture, to support and to accept. We talk about all kinds of things before a marriage that are practical and need to be talked about, but we seem to lack a meaningful dialogue about the meaning of love to each one of us.

"Maureen, I splot you." "What the hell do you mean?" "Well, I'm glad you asked...."

What we know is what we grew up with—our parents' version of love, mixed in with messages from the culture, through TV, movies, songs, books, and the like. Let's call it "Formula P." We grew up believing in our heart of hearts, because it's all we saw and experienced, that Formula P was love. But it may have been violence, drama, coercion, competition, control, manipulation, codependence, or neglect.

We—in our innocence—believed that was "love." Today, we give that same thing and expect to get it. If we were the subject of our parent(s') alternating control and affection, we tend to duplicate that in our intimate relationships. We call it love. We think it should work.

The truth is we all have our own definition of the word love and of everything that goes, or should go, with it. Not exploring this leads to trouble.

76. SOME SAY THEY WANT LOVE WHEN THEY REALLY WANT SAFETY.

IN THE FAMOUS "HIERARCHY OF NEEDS" developed by psychotherapist Abraham Maslow, the human priorities are mapped out. Maslow said that there is a relative strength of needs and that certain of those must be fulfilled before others, farther up the pyramid, are tended to. For instance, both hunger and friendship are needs that call for satisfaction. When you are very hungry, you will satisfy that need first, and then turn to your friend. Needs at a lower, more primal level must be satisfied before we can act to satisfy higher level needs.

The hierarchy, simply and generally, goes like this: survival, safety, affiliation/love, esteem, cognitive learning, aesthetic needs, self-actualization and, finally, the need for transcendence or discovering life's meaning. Survival is our most primal need and the first taken care of; transcendence the highest.

Let's focus on the first four: survival, safety, affiliation/love, and esteem. After the survival needs for food, water, and body maintenance are taken care of, we move on to safety: to feel secure, physically and emotionally safe, free of pain, and free to seek pleasure. After those needs have been met—and this is both short- and long-term—we want to affiliate with others, form friendships, fall in love, feel accepted, and exchange more intimate attention. Then we will move on to competency, achievement, peer approval, and mastery of a craft or profession.

Between safety and love, there is a lingering gap. We often look to belonging needs and love needs before we have completely satisfied our need to feel secure and emotionally safe. We are in pain and afraid, and we seek love and friendship with a request and a promise.

We are requesting that are partner make us feel safe. And we promise that we are able to give of love and ourselves completely.

But neither is true. No one else can meet your need to feel secure and safe, and, until you do, you cannot give fully of yourself in love.

Take care of your deep and important needs to feel safe and secure in yourself, and then seek out a meaningful relationship.

77. TO BE IN LOVE MEANS TO WALK IN THE FOREST OF THE UNKNOWN.

LOVE IS MAGELLAN, De Soto, Columbus, Lewis and Clark, and Neil Armstrong: love is an explorer. Fueled by a passion for searching, uncovering, and examining the new, love needs a little mystery. Deep love needs the unknown like a shark needs to keep moving in the water. A sideways glance at your partner is more intriguing than a stare. A glimpse in the shadows makes a heart race more than a full look in the daylight. The unknown pulls us toward it. When everything becomes known, when everything becomes habitual and predictable, love becomes a couch potato; it stagnates.

Still, love is paradoxical, and here is further paradox: while mystery tugs at a heart like a shiny lure in a creek, love needs a home in the known, too. We cannot love for long if we feel completely lost. We need some security, reference points, map checks along the way…some reassurance, so we can continue on the journey to know another and to know ourselves.

The wise couple recognizes that there needs to be a balance between the known and the unknown, between security and mystery, even if the mystery is, simply and beautifully, "What are the two of us going to be tomorrow?"

78. THE APPRECIATION OF DIFFERENCES IS THE FOUNDATION OF INTIMACY.

THE PSYCHIATRIST FRITZ PERLS first brought this to my attention. We love people who are similar to us, but not too similar. We love people who are different from us, but not too different. The process of becoming intimate is dependent on the discovery, acceptance, and appreciation of those differences.

What we do instead is try to make people like we want them to be. The kind of thinking that leads to this is an elaborate, self-contained "bible" of what is right and what is wrong.

We want to have the right kind of husband who has the right kind of job and makes the right amount of money; he speaks in the right way, listens in the right way, makes the right decisions, drives the right car in the right way, and makes love ever so rightly. And if he doesn't, well, we'll change him.

Appreciating differences means dropping this way of thinking. It means that you do not have "God in your pocket," who continually tells you what is right and what is not. It means seeing another person over there across from you who has a different past than you do and a different future. He has a life path and a destiny that is meant to be lived out, and he is doing his best to do that every day.

A large part of intimacy means being humble enough to look at someone else's way and learn from it, instead of insisting that something be done or expressed the way you do it.

The person whose slogan is "My way or the highway" is going to end up alone.

79. ROMANTIC LOVE IS BASED IN A KIND OF NARCISSISM.

THE PERSON WE SEE AND LOVE, through our rose-colored glasses, resembles ourselves. We look for someone who is different enough, but not so different that we can't find a piece of ourselves or our family in them... looks, qualities, ways of being, values.

This finding of someone similar (which is why we fall in love with the girl next door of the same age more readily than we do someone ten years older from another country) affirms our own sense of self on a continual basis. We idealize our loves just as we have idealized ourselves, seeing only the qualities that we want and find attractive. We see what we ourselves put "into the light" and choose not to see what is in the darkness, what some therapists call our shadow side. We all have the tendency to idealize that which we love, and often we defend that as vigorously as we defend our own self-image.

The feeling you have looking at your own child underlines this point. One of the reasons you are so enamored with your boy or girl is that you can see yourself in them. He or she is a little you or, at least, a little bit of you. The same is true of your mate.

80. WHEN YOU ARE IN LOVE, YOU ARE SEEING EACH OTHER AT YOUR BEST.

THIS IS TRUE for two important reasons: when I am courting you and falling in love with you, I am showing you my best, just as a male bird shows off its brightest plumage. Second, when each of us is falling in love, our physical and emotional chemistry changes, and we don't want to see anything that would dissuade us from seeing our partner as the most lovable person in the world. In other words, love is blind. For accuracy, I'd rather say infatuation is blinding, but it just doesn't sound the same, does it?

Many of us find out just how blinding infatuation is at the tail end of the relationship, when we recite the ever-popular phrase: "What did I ever see in him?" This phrase reflects our change of vision and points to the rose-colored glasses we once wore, which have now slipped down our nose a bit.

This is not to say that all love leads to disillusion and pain. It is a reminder to pay attention to our illusions and expectations. Desire blinds us. Fear blinds us. Our vision is obscured by many veils, especially when we are under the spell of the person we believe to be the love of our life.

Knowing this about ourselves, we can call forth our clarity, our wisdom, and our reasons for forming long-term, intimate relationships. It's also a vote for long courtships.

81. PASSION IS A FALSE GOD.

PASSION IS A SWEET ELIXIR. It is a universal sexual ideal. It is part of our essential recipe for feeling good. We are panicked when we think we have lost it. We often take very strange journeys in order to find it. We call passion out as one of the hallmarks of a good relationship. We strive to keep it alive.

By its nature, passion is stimulated by a swinging from one pole to another, just as a child on a playground swing swoops back and forth. And, just as the swing's arc gets smaller and smaller and eventually comes to rest, so does passion—unless someone at one end of the arc is pushing it. So it is in relationships.

A passionate joining is dependent on a passionate separation. The way we swing to fiery merger is to experience explosive departure (or threaten it). Distance fuels passionate closeness. Separation lights the lamp of joining as if you would never part again.

The couple that is unexpectedly separated, that quarrels often, that has dramatic fights, or that builds threats or drama into a relationship, may keep passion alive. But passion is a hungry god, not easily satisfied, and eventually it needs more drama, more chaos, and more violence to fuel itself. Then passion controls the relationship, instead of the individuals mastering passion.

Passion consumes itself. It is a fire that burns out in day-to-day existence. The duration of the relationship, extended togetherness, habit, familiarity—all these throw water on the fire of passion. Passion is replaced in many relationships by a different kind of intimacy, based on enthusiasm for your own life, harmony within the relationship, the vitality of a love kept alive, and tending to priorities outside of the relationship.

Chasing passion for its own sake is a false pursuit. Keep yourself alive, awake, and aware of life around you, and your natural vitality will be enough.

82. COMPASSION IS A KEY TO INTIMACY.

YOU CAN'T SAY that you have truly loved another unless you have a sense of compassion for them. Compassion, which Buddhists call our highest and most necessary kind of feeling, means that we can separate from our own self-interests and feel fully with someone else. We can feel their pain, their joy, their anger, and their sadness. We know something of what it is like to be inside their skin, and we can let them know that. Without compassion, you may have mutual attraction, compatibility, and a successful life together, but you won't have a deep love.

Compassion requires that you see the other person fully, that you have context and perspective and can see that they are part of the human condition. Compassion calls for a "bigness," a soul that is large enough to take in what others may find unacceptable or wrong in some way.

When you develop compassion for a romantic partner, it means you can separate your own interests and desires from who your partner is on his own. You can "see" at least part of his life path—where he has been and where he may be going—and separate that, if necessary, from your own.

Some of us grow up compassionate because it was part of our emotional heritage as a child. Others must learn to be larger inside and feel truly with another person.

83. YOU CANNOT BE LOVED UNLESS YOU ARE KNOWN.

ALTHOUGH LOVING RELATIONSHIPS THRIVE on a recipe that includes the unknown, curiosity, and a little bit of mystery, you cannot fully love another unless you know who they are. We all make choices, every day, about how much we will be known.

We ask ourselves: "Okay, if I tell him this, will he still love me?" Although we usually say "still like me" or "go away from me" or "get mad at me." But, at the core, we are afraid we won't be loved if we reveal all that we really are. So we hide—we hide those bits and pieces of ourselves that we consider ugly, unlovable, undeserving, or imperfect. For the person who does this to a great extent, there is always the lingering question: "Would he love me if he really knew me?"

I believe we all want the answer to that question. We want to be known. We want to be fully revealed and loved for it. But fear stands in the way, fear that says: "I can't really say that," "I can't look that way," "I can't let him know this," or "I can't act that way."

This is subtle and pervasive. There are little everyday examples and large, lifelong examples of how you will not reveal yourself out of fear and shame. Like many things in life and love, this is paradoxical. Whether we realize this or not, we have chosen our mate, in part, in order to know and resolve our "darker side"—that is, the parts we are not acquainted with fully, the qualities we deny. And while we devote energy to hiding them, these are the very "secrets" that will make us whole, will make us more human, more lovable and able to love.

Love is a result of revealing yourself.

84. RESPECT IS AT THE CORE OF ANY LASTING RELATIONSHIP.

RESPECT ISN'T AS FLAMBOYANT as love, but it's absolutely vital to a good relationship. Respect is the engine that drives love's car. Without respect, love is stuck on the side of the freeway.

To be respected is to be seen for who you are and admired, held in high esteem, and honored. We often have respect for things in other people that we find lacking or difficult in ourselves, such as self-discipline, will power, risk taking—qualities that we somehow envy and want a part of for ourselves. We commonly respect people for their courage and/or determination to overcome odds. We can respect whole groups of people, certain individuals, or just qualities in an individual. Our ability to respect has a great deal with our ability to love, because, as with love, respecting others grows out of being able to respect ourselves.

To look at our partner with respect includes a certain amount of awe, which enhances our feelings of love and affection. Conversely, to not respect your partner would mean you thought less of them than your ideal, or less of them than yourself. It would indicate a relationship where you felt more parental or caregiving.

Mutual respect, where you and your partner are actively responding to each other with admiration of some kind, gives your love substance, richness, and depth that it would otherwise lack.

85. LOVE HIDES BEFORE IT GOES AWAY.

WHEN WE LOSE LOVE, it's not as if we walk out into our rose garden one morning and it's been completely taken over by grass and weeds. If you see it that way, you've been asleep for a long time.

There are weeds in love's garden that are identified early on and dealt with. Some common weeds are secrecy, betrayal of trust, blame, too much anger, unresolved conflict, controlling another, excessive judgments, and deadening habit. When these things are spotted, get out the hoe and the weed killer. Left to grow, the weeds of blame, resentment, and control will slowly take over the garden.

Love rarely goes away dramatically, in one fell swoop. Love unravels gradually, much the way it takes form. There are stages of falling out of love, and, for the most part, we begin to retreat and hide our feelings from one another before making some kind of announcement.

It doesn't need to happen this way. Keep a watchful eye on the weeds in your relationship, and tend to them. Say the hard things— the things you are afraid of and believe you don't have to say. When you begin to hide from one another, love begins to die.

86. FORGIVENESS IS A SECRET OF LASTING LOVE.

EACH AND EVERY ONE OF US makes what we commonly call mistakes. We do something that hurts someone we love, just as someone we love has done something to hurt us. The nature of love is that we are vulnerable to each other.

Forgiveness is a conscious act. It is inner work in which we allow to pass out of us the pain we feel as a result of someone's actions in the past. Forgiveness is letting go of the past and turning our full attention to the present.

Forgiveness is not only an absolution and letting go that you do for someone else; it is also very much for ourselves. For some of us, the most important job we have to do is forgive ourselves for past transgressions. But even when someone else committed the painful act, forgiveness is for you because it frees you. When you let go and forgive another, you are free to move on and fully love. It's as if you took a large rock out of a stream and the stream was free to flow again in all its fullness.

The inner work you do to forgive takes you out of a victim's position. You no longer think of yourself as a passive or powerless, but as an active, powerful person getting on with your life and love. Forgiveness is good for your self-esteem, too, for you see yourself as spiritually larger and able to give something you value.

It is sometimes very hard work, no doubt. But the alternative is to remain stuck in the past or to move through life carrying a very large weight. It can be a telling question about your relationships to ask: "What have I not forgiven you for?"

Forgiveness is a gift…to another, to yourself, and to your relationship. It is what allows the love between you to flow.

THE HEART OF RELATIONSHIPS   127

87. COMMUNICATIONS IS THE FORM LOVE TAKES.

WE EACH HAVE A CERTAIN AMOUNT OF ROOM inside ourselves to receive love. We each have a certain capacity or potential for giving love. In each and every case, this potential is not known to someone else unless we make it known—unless we communicate.

So love can be seen as the part of the "psychic size" of a person and communications the outer manifestation of that size. By "psychic size," I mean the size of the soul—the mental, emotional, and spiritual space the other person has for relationships with others. Some of us are much larger than others.

We communicate in many, many ways: by what we say and don't say, by being with or away from, with our voice, with our attention, with our curiosity and our care, by giving gifts, by providing something the other needs, by responding to requests, by including the other…all of these and more are ways of communicating our love.

Each of these acts has three facets: a foundation or a capacity in ourselves, a form, and a result in another. We may have a capacity to give and receive love and fail to communicate it. We may try to communicate it and have it turned away. We may be with someone who is not able to return our love in a similar way. Or, over a long period of time, we may discover that our partner cannot truly receive what we have to give.

What happens in our relationships is the result of the capacity we have to love, our ability to communicate it, and the capacity of the other to receive and accept it.

As the outward manifestation of love, communication is the easiest part of the equation to pay attention to. By continually improving our communication skills, each of us can improve the form our loving takes. As our communication becomes more and more clear, more of the self is revealed, enlarging our capacity to love.

88. IN LOVE, YOU GIVE WHAT YOU THINK YOU HAVE THE MOST OF.

MOST OF US BELIEVE that love is about giving and not about taking. Giving is "better" than receiving—that's what we grow up hearing. So we give. Love is like a river flowing to the sea, like a searchlight shining on the object of its love, like the flower surrendering its pollen to the bee. All of these metaphors suggest a flowing out from one person to another.

What we give is different for each one of us. We may give material goods, our physical body, services, attention, devotion, feedback, advice, praise, support, and challenge. We may also give answers, ideas of right and wrong, values, manipulation, control, and violence. We give these in the name of love, too.

We will give what we believe we have the most of. If we have a lot of sexual energy, we will give that; a lot of money, we will give that; a lot of ideas, a lot of attention, a desire to please, a lot of advice about right and wrong, we will give it. We will give it because it is what we have to give; it is our way of loving. You cannot give what you do not have, and you will not give what you don't have enough of.

Giving is tricky business, like helping. Sometimes we will give regardless of what the other needs. Sometimes we want the other to give what they don't have.

I think about a way of loving that does not revolve around the polarity of giving and taking, but of fully being—a love where there is no consciousness of giving something or receiving something. It is more like two searchlights existing alongside one another: by the nature of what they do, they shine on each other. Try it. Just be who you are without reference to giving. Don't give, and don't take. Just be. See what happens.

89. A DEEP RELATIONSHIP BRINGS YOUR UNRESOLVED ISSUES TO THE SURFACE.

YES, LOVE CAN HEAL US, can help us grow, but when we are truly intimate with another, our fear, rage, desire, and unresolved needs also come roaring to the surface. In that state, we often run from love (or are run from) before we get the chance to heal. And then we repeat the cycle with someone else. We then come to believe that love will not heal us, and that, indeed, love will only hurt.

The truth is that a deep relationship is an emotional laser beam, and we are very ambivalent about such a searchlight into our soul. Do you really want to be known...every bit of you?

Intimacy will bring all of your issues to the surface. Here's how: we bring our history with us—the history that says things like, "I really don't feel lovable" or, "I want someone to take care of me" or, "I can't tolerate criticism." These hang around but don't come out in superficial relationships. But when we fall in love, the story changes. The childhood issues that have lurked back there in the swamp now come tumbling to the fore, once that we have gotten really close to someone. They poke their ugly, needy little heads into our nice, loving relationship and threaten to screw everything up. They must emerge if you are to be healed and wholly love another. Love wants to heal, but in order for it to heal, these nasty little issues must be brought into the light.

Being loved is about being known, even the characteristics, fears, and needs you find least admirable.

90. WE ALL VARY IN OUR CAPACITY TO GIVE AND RECEIVE LOVE.

DON'T BE FOOLED INTO THINKING that we all love in the same way. "I love you" is a relative statement. Each of us has a limited capacity for giving energy to intimate relationships and for what we can fully take in from another.

What follows is one way to look at a continuum of the quality of such relationships and give some definition to our limits. These do not define all relationships, but may help you reflect on yours.

Restricted love. This love is usually inadequate for both individuals involved, but they may remain in the relationship anyway. It is marked by fear, anger, frequent conflict, psychological pain, and sometimes physical abuse. Repeated separation and dramatic reunion may be a part of this relationship. Defensiveness is high, and few important needs are met. Individuals may believe this is all they're capable of and that they won't be able to find "a better love" elsewhere.

Deprived love. This relationship has moments of intimacy, but is laced with periods of detachment, alienation, passivity, and feelings of rejection for both partners. It could be characterized as empty, and the people involved often suffer from depression. Conflict resolution is problematic. Neither person has known a completely fulfilling love in childhood. Neither feels very capable of loving.

Divided love. Ambivalence about one's part in the relationship or about one's partner marks this kind of relationship. Divided love is also marked by open communication, bonding, and times of genuine comfort and closeness with each other. But there are equal parts of fear, attack, and unresolved conflict. Commitment is often an issue. A relationship of this sort can last for years and suddenly break apart, each partner going his or her separate way.

Whole love. Deep bonding needs are met in this relationship, and it is characterized by consistency, intimate communication, commitment, and trust. Conflict is present but is viewed as something to be quickly resolved and left in the past. There is an equity of give and take in emotional and physical loving. The individuals in this couple know themselves and each other.

To a large degree, these types of love, or relationships, are duplications of the kinds of love the individuals in the couple experienced as small children. Conditional love, alienation, or violence in childhood makes whole love in adulthood difficult, although not impossible.

91. ONE OF THE REASONS YOU LOVE HIM: HE REPRESENTS SOMETHING YOU WANT TO BE.

THERE'S AN OLD LINE about women having sex with powerful men: they have sex with the power and not the man. It's put rather crudely and contains a germ of truth. Often, we will seek out people who have an ample supply of some quality or characteristic we find lacking.

An indecisive man seeks out a strong, decisive woman. A weak and insecure woman is drawn to a man with power and confidence. A woman unsure of her parenting skills marries a man she is sure will be a good father. A man afraid to reveal himself pursues a woman who is open and articulate. Thus we "bring into the fold" of the relationship the quality we need to round out our own personality, using the strength of the other person to supplement our weakness.

One way to examine this in your own relationship is to look at the functions you perform for the couple or for the family. One of the more obvious, and traditional, ways of looking at this is through "work" roles...cooking, cleaning, fixing things, child care, managing the money, and so on. In most societies, these are broken down along gender lines, and they spawn a lot of jokes about bachelors on their own not being able to clean, sew, iron, or cook their own food. Therefore, they need a woman.

There are much more subtle and equally important roles and functions we perform that affect our intimate relationships. One partner may make all the social contacts for the couple. One may handle all the relationships with creditors and businesses. One may enforce norms and religious and moral issues.

One person may be much more sensitive to children and their issues. One may always take the lead in sexual contact and exploration.

Couples will often informally "assign" areas of their relationship to one another and make little jokes about that. "Oh, that's her department." "You should ask him about that; he handles all our _____."

The trade-off in this kind of relationship is that the absent quality in one of the partners does not blossom because it is always taken care of by the other. Thus we remain incomplete, supplemented by our partner.

Although division of labor may be perfectly healthy, most men and women today want relationships wherein one whole person engages another whole person.

92. SEEKING CONTROL, YOU WILL NOT FIND LOVE.

LOOKING AT MANY RELATIONSHIPS, it's difficult to tell whether the individuals in them want love or victory. If you were a fly on the wall and watched the continuing behavior of some couples, you would rapidly conclude that their relationship is about winning or losing. Many relationships are power struggles, not mutual exchanges of love.

This is something most of us would deny, but the truth is that many of us come into a relationship—any relationship—with the unconscious (or conscious) agenda to be in control. Those who seek control do so out of a lack of trust. They are afraid of what will happen if they do not control. Control is born out of fear. Fear stands in the way of love.

Control takes many forms: manipulation, hiding the truth, coercion, withholding affection or praise, controlling financial resources, controlling information, physical and emotional violence, prohibiting success, controlling the environment, competition, and threats to withdraw or abandon.

Being in a relationship where your partner is heavily invested in control is not pleasant and not easy to get out of. But sometimes getting out of it is the only way to get someone to face the fact that fear and control are strangling any love in the relationship. Even then, the fearful, controlling person may not invest in their own discovery and healing, but simply find another relationship to control.

93. A LOVE THAT IS EXTRAORDINARY DEMANDS A PRICE THAT MOST OF US ARE UNWILLING TO PAY.

FALLING IN LOVE WITH SOMEONE is the easy part. It's fun, exciting, and, like actual falling, is mostly effortless. Loving someone and building a powerful relationship asks much more: intention, skills, dedication, risk, time, and energy.

Most people go through a fairly predictable pattern in love relationships: they are attracted, fall in love, and then settle into a routine way of life that allows them each to have a partner and go on with their career or other interests. We are all susceptible to this: finding a mate and, once the relationship seems stable, expecting it to run along smoothly without maintenance.

We learn, however, that relationships are not like new cars that will run for 100,000 miles without a tune-up. Often this is a rude awakening.

"Big loves" thrive on the fact that the relationship itself is a priority and that the partners have the explicit intention of having an extraordinary relationship. It requires sophisticated communications skills. It asks for a dedication to detail and nuance. It challenges us to risk and face our worst fears. It needs time and space, just for the two of you. It requires an inordinate amount of energy, sometimes more than we think we have. And it means knowing that an extraordinary love is not going to just happen without intention and work.

But if you take the view that love is what we're here for, there is little else to do but roll up your sleeves and get to work.

94. THE WAY WE LOVE CHANGES AS WE GROW.

MOST OF US BELIEVE that when we enter a deep, loving relationship—which many of us equate with marriage—that it will last forever and that love will be the same for the duration. We pledge "forever," both informally and in our formal vows to each other. The "forever" is the reason, the guarantee, to which we allow ourselves to surrender.

Would you give your heart and soul to someone who said to you: "I know this isn't going to last long, but why don't we give it all we've got for a few months (minutes, years)?" Would you surrender?

Some of us do. Some of the brave among us (or foolhardy, depending on your point of view) are willing to surrender their hearts, knowing that the intense love they feel is not going to last, knowing that they will have a limited time with the person in front of them.

The fact is, the way we love originally, as young people and at the beginning of a relationship, does not last forever. Infatuation passes, we learn more about ourselves and our partner, stress and crisis invade the relationship, and our love is tested, then deepens or crumbles. The way we love changes, and the way we are loved changes, too.

The good news is that there is always something to learn about loving, some way to grow, and some way to deepen our own loving experience.

95. IF LOVE IS TO REMAIN LOVE, ONE THING IS ESSENTIAL: THE TRUTH.

"LOVE REJOICES IN THE TRUTH," is how the Bible says it. Subterfuge, secrecy, withholding, and manipulation all put love in a choke hold. Love thrives on openness and truth telling; in fact, the truth is a necessary condition for love. Otherwise we are dealing with illusion or the manufacturing of a personal image that the other is fooled by. The eventual loss of this illusion and revealing of the truth is the cause of a lot of our pain.

Love moves toward knowing the truth just as a plant turns and moves to the sunlight. We move toward another in order to find out who they are and in order to find out who we are. This search for knowing the other and ourselves cannot happen without the truth. In a real sense, we are explorers, and we are trudging through the jungles of our psyches to see them fully revealed. We do this in relationship to someone we love.

In a tenuous relationship, partners break apart if they discover some previously untold truth they can't tolerate. In a deeply committed relationship, the discovery of an unpleasant truth becomes grist for the mill and is consciously used to gain understanding of your partner and yourself.

The truth is absolutely essential.

96. THE SECRET TO BEING LOVED LIES IN NOT NEEDING IT.

WHEN I BADLY NEED LOVE and put my energy into being loved, I am trying to change someone else's behavior. This trying to change another is a risky business in any area of human behavior, but especially foolish in love. I am trying to be a salesperson for myself and persuade another person to devote their life to me.

Needing the love of your partner puts a drain on the relationship, almost like a tap on a maple tree that steadily removes the sap from the tree. You're saying to your partner, "Give me what I need," which usually continues with, "and I'll give you what you need." This is the sort of transaction that makes up a codependent relationship. This mutual meeting of needs may endure, but the relationship is usually fragile and gets into deep trouble when one person no longer needs what the other is giving.

The healthier place to put your energy is into loving—into learning how you can get bigger inside and become more of a loving person. This is the only part of the transaction you can control: your own thoughts, feelings, and behavior. It is your responsibility and yours only to deal with your own ability to love.

What the other person does with their energy and their way of loving is up to them. You may or not be the object of their love, but that, in a real way, is beside the point. Their loving is their business, and you have very little control of it. Your partner is living out his or her own way of being and loving.

Your way of loving is your business. Take care of your own loving, and drop your desire to be loved. It is liberating to let go of how your partner loves you.

97. WE TRY TO CONTROL LOVE BY BEING GOOD.

THIS IS ONE OF THE WAYS we try to control the flow of love in our relationships: we try to control the image of ourselves as a good person. There are two key words in that sentence—"image" and "good." We try to control the image of ourselves in the other's eyes, and we try to keep the definition of that image "good."

In other words, I control my own behavior and feelings with you, so I can put in front of you an ongoing movie of a good, lovable partner. In that way, I attempt to control the love I receive.

Here is what we believe: as long as we are "good," our partner will love us. If we are "bad," love will be withdrawn, or we will be punished in some other way. This is a conditional love, because the love is dependent on certain conditions being met. "Good" is one of those elusive words, but in most intimate relationships there is an operating definition that both people agree on. It usually means things like: happy, upbeat, supportive, loving, polite, attentive, and unselfish. Behavior or moods that are not "good" probably include: sad, mad, rude, self-centered, withdrawn, and uncaring. Our shadow does not come into the light.

We learn this at our parents' side before we go to school. Moms and dads drill us with the imperatives: "Be a good boy now." "Good little girls don't do that." "It's not polite to get angry." "Big boys don't cry." "Be nice." "Be a sweet little lady." Then we are rewarded for that prescribed behavior and are punished or feel disapproved of when we falter.

To be separated from our parents' love as a young person is one of our most severe threats, and when we fall into the "bad" side, we risk that very loss. We fear that Mom or Dad will take their love away.

Many of us repeat this pattern as adults, and we try to hold on to our partner's love by denying the "darker" side of our personalities. The cost for this is high. We give up our own authenticity. We give up knowing ourselves fully. And we give up the knowledge that someone loves us for who we are, in total, questions of "good" and "bad" aside.

It is much more worthwhile to put your energy into becoming your natural, authentic self.

98. "I NEED YOU" IS NOT THE SAME AS "I LOVE YOU."

OBVIOUS, RIGHT? Yet so many of us begin and maintain relationships based on need, either our own or someone else's, and think it means love. Needing someone is not inherently unhealthy; we all need. What throws a wrench in the works is when need is the dominant energy in the relationship. One of us then slips into manipulation, coercion, and control.

"I need you to be more affectionate." "I need you to be a good father." "I need you to let me know where you are." "I need you to be home more." "I need you, don't leave me." These may be legitimate expressions of a person's feelings or desires, and they may hook us into a kind of closeness, but they are not expressions of love.

Two people who need each other more than they love each other define the codependent relationship, which so easily gets in trouble in time of stressful events or crises. Any relationship based on a high level of need is fragile.

99. INTIMACY IS NOT A MYSTERY.

THERE IS NOTHING MYSTERIOUS about being intimate or close to another person. Granted, it sometimes seems a mystery, and we are often confused about our partners or ourselves. But the objective eye can see how intimacy happens, what goes into it, and why some relationships are not intimate.

Intimacy is the result of disclosure. There are other important factors, but primarily, intimacy depends on the quality and quantity of information exchanged.

All of us have relationships that vary in emotional depth and closeness. Our interactions and our ongoing relationships are on a spectrum from superficial to intimate. What follows is a summary of ways we relate to each other.

In superficial relationships, we learn very little about how the other person sees herself or wishes to be. We don't see the other for who they are; rather, they are seen as a way for us to get our own needs met. The topics we talk about are important to neither of us directly or perhaps to only one of us. We generalize and trade judgments about others. We usually talk about the past or the future, rarely the present. Feelings are seen as disruptive and awkward in superficial relationships and are usually avoided, especially about each other. What we say is usually remote from our own direct experience. Risks are not usually taken. One or both parties are often trying to convince, persuade, or coerce the other to think like they do or behave in a certain way. In this kind of relationship, conflict is avoided and open conflict easily leads to rupture of the relationship.

In intimate relationships, the topics we talk about are important to you and me or our relationship. The here and now is vital, and we disclose our present time experience…thoughts, feelings, wants, and needs. Feelings are seen as valuable, natural, and desirable and are easily shared or sought out by the other. The things we discuss are specific reports from our own experience. Personal autonomy is highly respected, as is personal responsibility; there is little attempt to persuade or manipulate. Competition is usually absent. Risks are seen as valuable, and there is an underlying trust that conflicts will be processed without punishment.

There. We can say what intimacy is. Can we do it?

100. INTIMACY IS, FIRST OF ALL, AN INTENTION.

INTENTION IS A BROAD AREA of human behavior that includes desire, need, fantasy, and willpower. We want things. We need things. We imagine and create things. We have, or don't have, the willingness to pursue those things. This is a broad and important area of our human experience.

We can have intentions whether or not we are conscious of them. When we are crystal clear about our intentions, we gain a new level of power. When we truly *intend* to be intimate, it is based on the beliefs that shared is better than solo, that collaboration is better than unilateral decision making, and that openness or self-revelation will lead us closer to love. If our basic intention is clouded on this matter of intimacy, or restrained by fear, we had best work with that first.

The most important thing you can say about building an intimate relationship is that you really want to. When you can say that, other things follow. If you can't say that with conviction, intimacy probably won't happen.

101. INTIMATES TRUST ONE ANOTHER, AFTER THEY TRUST THEMSELVES.

TRUST PRECEDES OPENNESS; openness builds trust. When I think about trust, I think much more about trusting myself as opposed to trusting someone else. When I trust myself deeply, I know that I can take the consequences of my own openness and my own behavior. Placing my trust in another is important, to be sure, but it follows self-trust. So intimates trust themselves and extend that trust to another.

I think of trust as a verb, which means it is a living, changing, active process between two people. It is fed and supported or it is chipped away and damaged. The erosion of trust is the beginning of the end of intimacy.

"Can I trust you?" is a very big question. "Can I trust myself?" is even bigger.

Trust is one of the most important issues we bring from our childhoods into our adult relationships. Believing that we are in a safe environment is one of our very first and most important lessons. We learn, in our first two years, to trust our own physical needs and responses and to trust that person with whom we're in our first relationship. We find answers to the questions: "Is what I'm feeling/wanting/needing valid, and is it responded to?" and, "Is it safe in here/out there/over there/with her?"

If we don't get that early sense of trust established, we often spend the rest of our lives looking for it. We ask the same questions in our adult relationships, and we are usually more conscious of discovering whether or not our partner is a person with whom we can safely and fully act out who we are.

Goethe wrote: "As soon as you trust yourself, you will know how to live." I believe him.

102. INTIMACY REQUIRES FREEDOM AND EQUAL AUTHORITY.

ONE OF THE MOST BASIC and beautiful things about being human is our ability to choose. Choosing implies that we have the freedom to imagine and select from a range of alternatives. If I do not feel free—free to discover my changing self, free to choose from a range of ideas and behaviors, free to drop my role, free to act the way I want to with you—we will not be intimate. We may remain in a close relationship, but we will not be truly intimate. Intimacy requires that each one of us have free choice about our own life and free choice about how we are with each other. This freedom leads to having an equal authority on how we live together—how we form the relationship, how we decide our lifestyle, and the other basic decisions we face as a couple. Freedom and personal authority in the relationship are a critical part of the dance of power and love.

103. INTIMACY THRIVES ON HUMOR.

WHENEVER I ASK ANY CLASS or workshop group to make a list of what they want in a mate, sense of humor is always in the top two. Humor saves our lives. Humor helps us deal with tragedy. Humor lightens our load. It is a relief valve. Humor lets us return to childhood for a while. Humor reveals how we look at the world.

Remember how it was when you first met your love? How you laughed? How you made fun of just about everything and everybody, including each other? It's part of our bonding to laugh with each other. Having a good laugh with a loved one is as good as a vacation.

Humor is also a very good way to get to know another person because it reveals the way they see themselves and how they look at the world. It is said that humor and tragedy are very closely related and sometimes depend only on our way of perceiving events around us.

When we shift the way we see an event and see that life is not as serious as we thought, the world looks less heavy and dark. A burden is lifted, and the load is lighter for our partners and ourselves.

So laugh; it's good for you.

104. LOVE IS NOT ENOUGH.

YEAH, THIS IS A TOUGH ONE. Sometimes, in spite of how much I care and am devoted to another person, the relationship just does not work. Love is love. A relationship working in "the real world" may be another issue.

We are happiest when we maintain our excitement, care, and responsiveness to another, and we work well together in the everyday tasks, conflicts, and crises that all of us will face. Some of us have the passion without the practicality, and it feels like a compelling, up-and-down relationship. Some of us work very well together, but the pizzazz is missing. Optimal relationships have some of both. Relationships, besides being loving and romantic, are practical, too, and must exist in the real world.

Don't get me wrong, love goes a long, long way, but despite the Beatles' words, it is not all we need. There are some other things in life that help a great deal, that give our love for one another a healthy garden in which to grow. A strong self-image, good communication skills, a significant degree of mental and physical health, a relatively low dose of disaster and back-breaking poverty, a commitment to the long term, a safe emotional environment, a willingness to share yourself, a sense of security…all these things give a couple a solid vessel in which to keep their love.

Do something about providing those things to support your love.

105. LOVE IS INFINITE AND ONGOING; OUR RELATIONSHIP WITH LOVE IS PROBLEMATIC.

I HAVE A VISION OF LOVE as an ongoing, infinite flow of energy that is always moving through the universe and through each of us. That flow of love is always there, always present, always accessible, and it will not end. Our choice is if and how we step into that flow and allow ourselves to love.

Time is finite; at least in my individual life I have a limited amount of it. I have x-number of years, and then I will die or take another form. Within my limited time here, I want to give myself to that flow of love as often and with as much commitment and consistency as I can muster. It seems wasteful to spend time out of love.

Appendix
The Ten Most Popular Myths
About Relationships

1. Two half-people come together to make a whole.

2. "Don't worry I can change him" or, "Don't worry, he'll change after we get married."

3. Your partner should know what you want.

4. If your partner really loved you, s/he would do what you want.

5. Marriage is a guarantee of security.

6. Power has nothing to do with love.

7. We all know what marriage is.

8. Passion is the most reliable predictor of success.

9. Your job is to meet your partner's needs.

10. Love stays the same.

About the Author

John Thomas Wood, PhD, is an author and artist living in the Pacific Northwest. The author of nine books on human behavior, he has devoted the last forty years of his life to empowering and encouraging individuals and organizations to reach their highest potential. During that time, he has served as a psychotherapist, university instructor, consultant, and workshop leader, working throughout the United States, Western Europe and in Mexico.

Dr. Wood spent seventeen years as a resident fellow at Center for Studies of the Person in La Jolla, California, working with Carl Rogers and other humanists to apply the ideas and practices of client-centered therapy to education, politics, health care, group therapy, international relations, and business. He has a special interest in the philosophy and practice of power and the use of power in personal relationships, families, and organizations.

As a consultant, Dr. Wood has worked in cross-cultural settings, universities, large business, health care, and varying levels of government. Over the past thirty years, he has traveled and worked throughout Europe and, for four years, led a program in the U.S. and Holland aimed at improving the person-to-person skills of physicians.

In addition to writing, he brings a unique perspective to the creation of digital artwork and has large fine-art prints hanging in homes and offices in this country and abroad.

ALSO BY JOHN THOMAS WOOD

The Heart of Feeling

The Heart of Power

The Heart of Fear

The Heart of Leadership

Be Strong, Be Smart

Discover more books and learn about our
new approach to publishing at **booktrope.com**.

Made in the USA
Lexington, KY
12 May 2015